A Traveller's Wine Guide to
SPAIN

A Traveller's Wine Guide to
SPAIN

By Harold Heckle

Text for the original edition
by the late Desmond Begg

Armchair Traveller
at the bookHaus

First published in Great Britain in 2012 by

The Armchair Traveller at the bookHaus
70 Cadogan Place
London SW1X 9AH

www.thearmchairtraveller.com

Copyright © Philip Clark Ltd, 2012
Design copyright © Interlink Publishing, 2012
Cover photo © Fernando Madariaga/ICEX
Map production: Julian Ramirez
Book design: James McDonald/The Impress Group

Originally published in the USA in 2012 by
Interlink Publishing, Northampton, Massachusetts

Traveller's Wine Guides series conceived by Philip Clark
Abbotsford, 14 Watts Road, Tavistock PL19 8LG, UK

ISBN 978-1-907973-03-1

A CIP catalogue for this book is available
from the British Library

Printed and bound in China

In memory of Desmond Begg,
the author of the first edition of this book,
whose premature passing represented a sad loss
to the world of wine writing

CONTENTS

Map of vineyards of Spain viii
How to use this book x
Wine touring xi

Introduction xiv
Visiting bodegas xiv
Hotels in Spain xv
Eating in Spain xvii
How to recognize your wine xviii
Driving in Spain xxi

Navarra 3
The wines of Navarra 5
Pamplona 7
Navarra's wine country 9
Food and festivals of Navarra 13
Where to stay and eat 15

Rioja 17
Rioja—the grapes 20
Rioja—the Bordeaux legacy 22
Rioja Baja 24
Logroño 26
Rioja Alta and Alavesa 28
Haro 33
Food and festivals of Rioja 35
Where to stay and eat 38

Aragón 41
Where to stay and eat 47

Northeast Spain 49
Catalonia 49
Barcelona 51
Other Catalan wine regions 57
Penedès and Cava 61
The Raimat Estate 69
Priorat and the mountains of Catalonia 71
Catalan cuisine 76
Where to stay and eat 78

Castile 81
Valladolid—the perfect hub 81
The wines of Castile 84

Toro 90
Rueda 92
The mountains of Segovia 94
The gastronomy of Castile 97
Where to stay and eat 100

The Southeast—Murcia 103
The wine regions of Murcia 105
Bullas 110
Yecla 111
Eating in Murcia 112
Where to stay and eat 113

Andalusia 115
Córdoba 117
Montilla 120
Málaga 124
From Málaga to Jerez 127
Sherry 129
Sherry and its traditions 132
Jerez de la Frontera 135
Food and festivals of Andalusia 143
Where to stay and eat 147

Northwest Spain 151
Galicia 151
The wines of Galicia 155
Albariño country 161
Ribeira Sacra 163
Heading South 168
Where to stay and eat 170

The Balearic and Canary Islands 173
The Balearics 174
The Canaries 176
Where to stay and eat 179

Glossary of useful food and wine terms 180
Principal grape varieties 184
Spanish vintages 186
Further information 187
Further reading 190
Index 192

BAY OF
BISCAY

Santander   Bilbao

ASTURIAS

BASQU
COUNT

Logroñ

R. Miño

Santiago de Compostela

THE RIO

GALICIA

OLD CASTILLE

Valladolid

R. Duer

Zamora

Segovia

Madrid

R. Tagus

NEW CASTIL

Alcázar de San Juan

EXTREMADURA

Valdepeñas

PORTUGAL

R. Guadiana

R. Guadalquiv

Cordoba

Seville   ANDALUSIA   Grana

Málaga

Jerez

CANARY ISLANDS

LANZAROTE

LA PALMA   TENERIFE   FUERTEVENTURA

Santa Cruz

LA GOMERA   Las Palmas

HIERRO   GRAN
CANARIA

MOROCCO

FRANCE

Pamplona

NAVARRA

Huesca

CATALONIA

Barcelona

R. Ebro

Lérida

Zaragoza

Tarragona

ARAGON

MENORCA

THE LEVANTE

Palma de Mallorca

MALLORCA

Valencia

IBIZA

THE BALEARICS

R. Júcar

MURCIA

Alicante

R. Segura

MEDITERRANEAN SEA

N
S   E
W

0   100   200   300

100   200

How to use this Book

This book is designed to give practical help to wine lovers travelling in Spain.

The chapters are designed to guide you around the different wine regions of Spain and introduce you to their delights. With its help, you will be guided through stunning countryside to some wineries I consider worthwhile visiting for reasons I hope you will discover as you use this book.

Advice about driving in Spain in the age of GPS technology may seem superfluous. Indeed, my first piece of advice is for you to acquire or rent such a device as soon as you can—it facilitates every aspect of touring Spain dramatically. Every car rental company has them available for hire for modest amounts and they can be set to English or (for the adventurous) Spanish. However, some general tourist information provided by this book should make your journey a far more personal and pleasurable wine appreciation experience.

Each chapter has a regional map, showing main cities, major wineries and an outline of the road system.

Useful Information

Details, which you may find useful, will accompany the text as it guides you through the various regions. These sections will give you an idea of the range of wineries (bodegas) that can be visited, together with some of their facilities and additional hints. In every case it is worth phoning first to ascertain how the land lies; Spaniards, and especially winemakers, live busy lives and prefer to hear of potential visits beforehand. Where possible, do look for additional hints online, as many bodegas' websites are frequently updated. At the end of each chapter you will find recommendations on hotels and restaurants.

The bodegas

Spain is the world's fourth largest wine producer. Hence a book such as this can only give an impression of what this large and colorful country can provide for the wine enthusiast. The selection of bodegas is wide, but it remains the author's personal selection.

In most if not all cases you will be well advised to make a reservation beforehand. The opening hours of bodegas are rarely a fixed thing. Telephone and email are the best forms of contact. A sample email in Spanish is given in the Reference section. Advice on how to use the phone in Spain is also provided. Bodegas often offer free tastings, but a subsequent purchase will always go down well.

Wine touring

Travelling to Spain is no longer the great expedition it used to be. To give you

(BLANCA BERLIN/ICEX)

The pilgrim route of St James crosses this ancient bridge at Puente de la Reina, Navarra

some idea of how popular it has become, no two countries in the world share more flights between them than the United Kingdom does with Spain. The ease with which it is possible to visit Spain by air has changed the way road travellers tackle getting to know the countryside. Most people fly to a destination in Spain and then rent a car before touring.

The purpose of this book is to simplify touring wine regions as much as possible.

Spain is a country rich in history and tradition, much of it linked to wine. It is also a prosperous land. Once a world superpower, it has in recent years flourished once again to become one of Europe's leading economies and a place with a determination to get things done. Spaniards have rediscovered a pride in all things Spanish: their history, their multi-layered and varied culture, their exuberant and noisy lifestyle, their fashion sense and, of course, their

Signed barrels decorate this restaurant entrance

(FERNANDO MADARIAGA/ICEX)

wine and cuisine.

Modern Spain likes to be compared with advanced countries around the world and today foreign influences are palpable in nearly all aspects of life. Still, a very tangible "Spanishness" pervades. The wine industry has also looked abroad and borrowed grape varieties and technology to enhance the quality of its output, while at the same time striving for unique character.

Most of Spain's wine regions are in the interior, in largely unspoiled countryside far from crowded coastal tourist destinations. Far removed from the ever more crowded Costas, Spain remains a fascinating country of historic cities, high mountain ranges and sweeping plateaux. A wine tour of Spain will reveal a range of cultural and gastronomic experiences that few beach holiday visitors would suspect existed. A wine traveller has the possibility of really getting to the heart of this large and beautiful country.

INTRODUCTION

S PAIN IS A COUNTRY with surprisingly ancient links
to wine. Estimates for the arrival of wine culture seem
constantly to be pushed back. Certainly wine was being
made, drunk and traded 2500 years ago as far inland as what
is now Valladolid. The coastal regions, particularly along the
Mediterranean, have had the longest wine influence.

Spain has nearly 1.2 million hectares (three million
acres) under vine, which gives it the largest area of vine
cultivation of any country in the world. Innovation and
improvement have affected many wine-producing parts of
Spain, and regions recognized for their excellence seem to
win official approval regularly. As I write, there are 81 areas
classified as producing quality wine within specific regions
(*denominaciones de origen* or DOs), of which four are quality
wines (*vinos de calidad*), nine are single estate wines (*vinos de
pago*) and the remainder designations of origin.

Cava, Spain's quality sparkling wine, is an exception in
that it may be made in many different regions but must
always adhere to bottle fermentation for the final phase of
its production, a process similar to that used north of Paris
to make Champagne.

The first authorized classifications date from 1932 when
the following DOs were created: Jerez-Xères-Sherry;
Manzanilla de Sanlúcar de Barrameda; Málaga; Montilla-
Moriles; Rioja; Tarragona; Priorato; Alella; Utiel Requena;
Valencia; Alicante; Ribeiro; Cariñena; Penedés; Condado
de Huelva; Valdepeñas; La Mancha; Navarra; and Rueda.
There are also over 40 table wine classifications able to use
the traditional *Vinos de la Tierra en España* (Spanish country
wines) labels.

Visiting bodegas

Historically, the best welcomes available to wine lovers in
Spain are to be found in Jerez and the other towns of the
Sherry Triangle (see pages 127–146).

Most leading firms have impressive, venerable wineries and they are proud to offer guided tours that end with tastings and can include an audiovisual presentation.

However, the Spanish wine industry has not yet fully woken up to wine tourism, so your enterprise will pay dividends. Relatively few bodegas give tours (though membership of a wine club or a wine appreciation society should help you).

Spaniards are a hospitable people. If you have taken the trouble to write or phone in advance you will be greeted with great courtesy. If you make appointments, be sure to keep them. If you are delayed, please phone to advise. Winemakers are busy business people these days.

Hotels in Spain

Since Spain emerged from the military dictatorship of General Francisco Franco it has undergone a remarkable transformation. The country has changed from being a beautiful but rather quaint place where people ran with bulls and threw tomatoes at each other to a dynamic, international powerhouse of democratic values and surprising financial muscle.

While Franco's Spain relied almost entirely on Sherry wine and tourism for foreign currency, today it is a cornerstone of modernity within the European Union with a very diverse economy.

As a consequence, while history plays a crucially important role in Spain, the future is definitely the most important element of a Spaniard's view of existence. Hence, you will find hotels that cater for both conceptions of the country. The country's remarkable range of Parador hotels hark back to Spain's glorious past, with a whiff of the puritan standards of Franco's time. There are also superb mid 20th century hotels built by foreign investors who rapidly understood Spain's undoubted tourist potential.

Equally, you will find amazing new hotels that cater for Spaniards' exacting standards of cleanliness and modernity, some sensitively set in historic locations. Among the country's remarkably reliable chains you'll find NH hotels, easily bookable online and always immaculately clean with a good value for money attitude to doing business.

Further upscale you'll find AC hotels (coincidentally owned and built by the man who originally began the NH chain before he sold it on). These hotels offer the same standard of impeccable presentation but strive to offer a more design-oriented experience. Some AC hotels have been built in old monasteries and other fascinating buildings.

At the other end of the range you will also find an amazing array of smaller, owner-run and designed *casa rural* (rural lodge) hotels that offer an intimate and more homely accommodation experience.

Few hotel industries on earth are as well thought out and carefully regulated as Spain's. Spaniards have a knack of making you feel at home, while sometimes at the same time appearing aloof and perhaps even a bit arrogant. The star system is remarkably uniform and totally trustworthy. One star will be basic; two stars will improve on that and may include an en-suite bathroom; three stars will always include a decent-sized bathroom and most facilities you would expect of a hotel, while four- and five-star hotels will match those of any other country, while outdoing many elsewhere.

Food may appear a bit "samey," with uniform flavors and a standard approach to preparation and presentation, but you will soon learn to appreciate the reliability at your disposal.

Having experienced Spain's hospitality once, the vast majority of tourists are keen to return to repeat the enjoyment. May your personal experience be further heightened by the county's best wines.

Hotel categories

Hotels in Spain maintain high standards that are regulated by law. Their category is immediately visible and prices should be easily verifiable. Most have online information and reservation facilities.

Accommodation categories include, in ascending order of price:

Fonda (F) Inn
Casa de Huespedes (CH) Guest House
Pension (P) Guest House

always expect you at lunchtime, not dinnertime.

Spanish cuisine

The Internet today provides food and wine lovers with a virtual cornucopia of references and access to endless publications. Even celebrity chefs such as Juan Mari Arzak and El Bulli's Ferrán Adriá have published fascinating books for the real expert.

I see Spain's food as divided in three. First, there are snacks such as *tapas*, *pintxos* or finger/bar food generally. Then you have the standard *Menú del Día* (menu of the day) restaurants that offer good value daily fare in every town and city of the land. Finally there is the amazing top flight of *Restaurantes de Autor*—chef-driven restaurants that earn multiple Michelin stars and currently head Europe and the world's culinary innovation stakes. Ferrán Adriá's El Bulli has been voted Best Restaurant in the World for several years running now, and he is just one member of a whole generation that has transformed how Spanish cuisine is perceived internationally.

My advice is to make sure you have the set breakfast—*Desayuno del Día*—which includes orange juice, toast or pastry and coffee for a special price.

For lunch do try the *menú del día*, including bread, wine, beer, a soft drink or water, an appetizer, a main course and either a dessert or coffee all included in a fixed price. But if you possibly can, try to experience one top end restaurant. It may be a memory you treasure forever.

How to recognize your wine

Spain produces less wine than either Italy or France despite having more land under vine. Its climate varies considerably from the north and west, where the influence is Atlantic, to the regions of the south and east, which are Mediterranean in character. The result is a wide variety of types of wine.

The progress achieved by Spain's wine industry has been impressive in recent years. To help foster improvements, Spanish authorities, encouraged by the European Union, maintain an official system to guarantee minimum levels of quality and provide guidance.

Denominaciones de Origen

Denominaciones de Origen, or Denominations of Origin (DOs), are similar to the French *Appellations Contrôlées* or Italian *Denominazioni di Origine*. In 1996 there were just 49 of these dotted around the country, and in 2001 there were 81. Each is overseen by a *Consejo Regulador* (CR) or Regulating Council.

Consejos Reguladores, Spain's regional watchdogs, oversee virtually every aspect of wine production and aging: they ensure wine is made from grapes grown within delimited areas; that it is made from authorized varieties; and that the wineries in which it is made are suitably equipped and maintain a legally set high standard of hygiene.

Consejos often reject wine that is considered to be of insufficient quality. This is then either sold off in bulk or distilled. Standards are exacting. Every bottle that meets quality standards is entitled to the coveted back label stipulating the DO.

The back label

The back label gives an indication of the aging process the wine has undergone. In general Spanish wines are divided into young *vino joven* (or *vino del año*), *crianzas*, *reservas* or *gran reservas* depending on how much aging they have been given in barrel and bottle. However, some iconoclastic producers make fine wines outside the DO network. These wines are not entitled to a *Consejo* back label. But most of the time an official back label is a guarantee of reliability and quality.

Hostal (Hs) More expensive than the foregoing, but still cheap by European standards.

Hostal Residencia (HsR) One, two or three stars. Do not serve meals.

Hotel (H) One to five stars.

Paradores These are mostly historic buildings, beautifully restored monuments, such as monasteries or castles. The concept dates from 1928 through former dictator Francisco Franco's years in government as a way of preserving ancient buildings. They are colorful and often high-end though they can sometimes be cheaper than the top hotels. Some are five star though some (eg Santillana del Mar and the Alhambra in Granada) rate three or four stars. Please consult the Paradores Nacionales website www.parador.es. Prices vary according to location and time of year. There are often discounted rates available, for example for the over 55s.

Eating in Spain

Food is taken very seriously in Spain. You pay for the quality you get. If a menu is cheap it may be delicious and nutritious, but it will not match the quality of products offered by an expensive selection. If you are on a budget make sure you check the menu displayed (usually on a board outside the restaurant) to ensure you don't exceed your limits, and remember that at lunchtime most restaurants offer a bargain daily menu, which you may need to ask for specifically. Also, even if you are on a tight budget, do leave enough in your funds to allow for at least one high-end meal so as to have an idea of what is really possible in terms of wine and food appreciation. Really good restaurants are almost always in demand, so do book ahead. Spaniards are not too shy to spend big money on wine and food and you should try to explore this scene at least once.

Please remember that the main meal in Spain is always at lunchtime. People take time over lunch and much business is conducted over the lunch table. Most businesses close and restaurants fill up from between 2 pm and 3 pm. Dinnertime will involve a lighter or tapas meal. If a Spaniard invites you to eat (*a comer*) they will

Rioja The name of the region.

Consejo Regulador de la Denominación de Origen Calificada Rioja The official logo of the *Consejo Regulador*, which regulates and guarantees the origin of the wine and its quality. Strict requirements for aging are laid down by the *Consejo Regulador*.

Crianza The indication of aging: *vino de crianza* is wine matured for at least one year in oak cask and a further period in bottle. It is normally released in its third year.

Reserva is a selected wine that has been aged for at least one year in oak and two or three in bottle. It is normally sold in its fourth year. Most top winemakers prefer to release their best wines as *reservas*.

Gran reserva is a wine made from a good vintage that has been aged for three years in oak cask and three in bottle. It is normally sold in its sixth year.

Wines with some oak aging (but below the standard set for *crianza*) are sometimes labeled *Roble* (oak).

Wines with little or no aging usually have the word *joven* (young) or *cosecha* (vintage) followed by the harvest date.

Driving in Spain

Since joining the European Union (EU), Spain has benefited from heavy investment in its transport systems.

Today, it has some of the best rail and airport facilities in the world. Roads too have been much improved, although you may still come across picturesque sections that remind you of days gone by.

There are some points worth bearing in mind. The EU and Spain have launched a major campaign to improve road safety so speed traps can be encountered almost anywhere. You can be stopped on the road or have a photograph of you speeding sent to your home address. Drunk driving is also heavily penalized, so it is important not to drink and drive.

Despite attempts to improve safety, Spain still has a relatively poor road safety record. In spite of strict drunk-driving laws, it is still quite common to see

View of Salnés Valley, Meaño, Galicia,
from Bodegas Agnusdei

roadside cafés at lunchtime packed with truck drivers drinking wine.

Do remember that after Switzerland, Spain is Europe's second most mountainous country, so driving requires special concentration.

When driving, please remember the following:

🚗 Drive on the right and observe road signs with attention. Signs will post the speed limit and other traffic notices. If there are no road signs, give way to traffic from the right.

🚗 Seatbelts are compulsory, including in the back seat.

🚗 You must have a regulation country sticker (eg GB) to show where your car is registered.

🚗 For your safety carry a breakdown triangle and a yellow reflective jacket.

(PHILIP CLARK)

 Always carry a spare tire and a jack, plus a spare set of headlight bulbs.

Make sure you are insured. If you are not, you may be fined.

The roads

For details on Spain's roads, weather conditions and hazard warnings, it is best to consult the government's road traffic authority: www.dgt.es

Roads in Spain can be quite busy, even main *Autopistas* (highways or motorways), on which you will be expected to pay a toll.

Documents

Wherever you go you are required to carry your national identification document at all times. On the road always carry this document (it could be a passport), driver's license and insurance.

Insurance

Consult your auto club or insurance company. It is worth increasing your insurance coverage (for yourself and for any passengers). The costs of litigation in Spain are high.

Driving tips

🚗 It is hard to avoid traffic jams in main cities, so avoid city traffic at rush hour.

🚗 Never leave your car unlocked and don't leave valuables visible. Where possible use hotel car parks, or guarded ones.

🚗 Truck drivers often indicate right when it is safe to overtake. If they then indicate left or stop indicating, there is oncoming traffic.

🚗 Watch the center line to see if you are allowed to overtake. If you do so when it is forbidden you could be fined.

Fines

Always have enough cash (you should always carry €150–200) to pay on-the-spot fines.

Speed Limits

Urban areas:
50 km/h (30 mph)
Normal roads:
90–100 km/h (56–62 mph)
Motorways:
120 km/h (74 mph)

How to get the best out of your trip to Spain

Every wine trip requires forward planning. The aim of this guide is to facilitate this, at the point of origin, and also to suggest ideas, routes and locations to smooth your way once on the road. Fine-tuning can be done on the hoof, but nothing can improve on the effects of a small amount of early research.

If you have not been able to plan ahead, then it is always worthwhile dedicating some time at the beginning of your journey to smooth the way ahead. In this guide you'll find phone numbers, email addresses and websites to help you with your forward planning.

Turning up unannounced at Spanish wineries can be a difficult business, as most if not all

(JUAN RAMÓN YUSTE/ICEX)

View of Ciga, Navarra

prefer to know if people are coming in order to cater for their needs. Many bodegas in this guide are small and even big ones, such as Vega Sicilia, need someone to travel especially to the winery to deal with guest arrivals.

So please try and plan ahead and arrange your visits with at least a few days' anticipation. If you don't advise of your arrival you may find that everyone has gone for a coffee break. And lunch can be a movable feast, starting at 2:30 or 4 pm and continuing for between two and four hours. So anticipated planning will help avoid frustration at both ends.

Booking ahead is particularly recommended when reserving hotel rooms during peak tourist seasons. Remember, if you are travelling with a car, make sure you book a garage space. Many Spanish hotels have limited parking space and it's always a good idea to have your own spot designated for easy alighting.

Internet access in Spain

Finding Internet access in Spain is simple. Most hotels provide it, some without charge. Many towns now provide free WiFi zones. In those that do not, some like the very un-Spanish Starbucks do so as a matter of course, and roadside newspaper kiosks are fast joining in this trend.

NAVARRA

NAVARRA WAS AN INDEPENDENT KINGDOM that reached the zenith of its power in the 11th century, when its kings ruled from Bordeaux in the north to Barcelona in the east. Through its valleys have marched a constant ebb and flow of conquering or retreating armies. Charlemagne forced the Moors southward through here. Carlist volunteers rallied in their thousands to the Nationalist cause during the Spanish Civil War. Blood has flowed here through the centuries.

Navarra is steeped in history. Pilgrims have crossed the northern part of the province en route to Santiago de Compostela since the Dark Ages, as numerous chapels and churches testify. If you cross over from France, I suggest you do so through the historic Pyrenean pass of Roncesvalles, made famous by the ancient epic poem *Chason de Roland* (the *Song of Roland*). You may wish to take in the French towns of Valcarlos and St Jean-Pied-de-Port en route.

Today Navarra is a prosperous province producing excellent farm products as well as wine. Its countryside can be viewed as a microcosm of Spain, with the Pyrenean mountains in the north descending to flat, dry plains in the south.

Pamplona

The ancient and historic capital of Navarra is a natural magnet for any wine traveller. American author Ernest Hemingway made this city and its annual Running of the Bulls festival famous in his novel *The Sun Also Rises*. Every July the whole city celebrates the **San Fermín festival**, a feast of red wine, bull running and bull fighting. A word of warning; San Fermín is not for the faint-hearted. Be prepared to stay up most of the night and get up early the

« A solitary pilgrim walks along the ancient route of St James at Abinzano, Navarra

3

NAVARRA

next morning to see the running of the bulls.

If you approach from the port or airport of Bilbao, do so by crossing the impressive Sierra de Cantabria mountain range via Vitoria. There are a number of small road crossings you can choose from; they are all worth exploring.

TO GET TO PAMPLONA

Pamplona is 160 km (100 miles) south of Bilbao, 80 km (50 miles) north of Logroño, 430 km (270 miles) northeast of Madrid.

The Wines of Navarra

The Denomination of Origin of Navarra covers some 17,340 hectares (42,000 acres) of vineyards between Pamplona and the mighty Ebro River. It is divided into five sub-regions: Valdizarbe around Puente la Reina; Baja Montaña on the Aragón border to the east; Tierra Estella around the town of Estella; Ribera Alta around Olite; and Ribera Baja around Cintruénigo and Tudela. The landscape dips as you move south leading to higher temperatures and lower rainfall.

Navarra was once the heartland of Spain's *rosado* (rosé) wine industry. Made mainly from the Garnacha grape variety, most of the country's summer rosés were produced here. In the late 1980s and 1990s much progress was made in quality red wine production. Today a rising flow of high quality reds and whites has been added to the already well-established range of *rosados*.

Navarra's reputation was built initially on the quality of the once much-maligned yet generously planted Garnacha grape, which thrives in the region. Picked ripe and macerated for only a short time to extract just a delicate amount of color from the skins, there can be little doubt that Garnacha produces some of the best *rosados* in Spain—richly pink in color, fruity and full of life. These rosés are dry—considerably drier than most of those made elsewhere in Europe—packing more mouth-feel, structure and complexity. Some traditional styles are aged in wood and yield a brick-to-yellow color and a subtle hint of oak.

(ICEX)

Harvesting by hand in Navarra, ripe grapes are carefully picked in the fall to ensure maximum quality

From the mid-1980s the region began to modernize. The phenomenal success of neighboring Rioja on the world market led Navarra to revolutionize its wine industry. With plenty of support and encouragement from the regional government, an investment and research program in wineries and vineyards was launched, the spectacular results of which are now available internationally.

Grape varieties

By the beginning of the 1990s the region's whites had got fruitier and crisper as a result of better, controlled fermentation. Well-made and carefully aged *crianzas* and even *reservas* also began to appear. Even the stalwart *rosados* improved as a result of better viticulture and vinification. New plantings of Tempranillo, Viura and even Cabernet Sauvignon and Chardonnay now form the basis of Navarra's modern wines.

Garnacha is still Navarra's leading grape variety, covering over 50 percent of vineyard area, with Tempranillo, Merlot,

Cabernet Sauvignon,
Viura and Chardonnay
making up most of the
rest. White varieties tend
to be planted on the higher
ground of Tierra de Estella
and Ribera Alta.

Today you can look
forward to bold and in-
teresting blends of grapes,
such as Chardonnay with
Viura, and Garnacha and
Tempranillo with Cabernet
Sauvignon. The range of
Navarra's wines, as well as
their quality, has improved
immeasurably, and there
can be little doubt that
winemaking here will con-
tinue to progress: it is still a
region to watch.

Most leading producers
welcome visitors and are
listed below. There are two,
however, that are not—the
first because it does not
accept visitors and the
second because a visit to its
winery involves a significant detour. So, look out
for the wines of Ochoa and
Bodegas Principe de Viana,
as they are well worth
tasting.

FOR FURTHER
INFORMATION
Please consult: www.
vinonavarra.com. This is the
website of The Consejo
Regulador Denominación

de Origen "Navarra," Calle
Rua Romana, s/n,
31390 Olite, Navarra
Tel: 948 741 812
Fax: 948 741 776
consejoregulador@vinonavarra.com

Pamplona

Any reader of Ernest
Hemingway's novels will
be able to tell you that this
city is best known for the
madness and sheer joy of
its two-week Feria de San
Fermín, the famous bull-
running and bull fighting
fiesta in July. In fact, **Hemingway's bust** decorates a
plaza outside Pamplona's
bullring. Look deeper and
you'll see a pulsating and
sophisticated regional
capital with a compact city
center of narrow streets
flanked by tall old houses
and more open modern
districts of wide avenues.
It has an attractive Gothic
cathedral, interesting gardens, an impressive fort,
the old Ciudadela, and a
good market.

Pamplona is not re-
nowned for its regional
food, and the town does
not house any bodegas.
The real secret lies in its
bars and restaurants where
you can find the greatest
range of regional wines.

One of the best ways to enjoy the city is to stroll around and take in some of the bars, eventually settling on an *asador* restaurant specializing in tasty and traditional oven-cooked dishes. These establishments serve roasts made up of generous portions of meat that have been grilled on open fires, accompanied by salad and vegetables. House wines may be served from earthenware jars and are usually pretty rough and ready. The wines of leading firms are a better bet and you will find them on the wine list. Do not hesitate to ask for recommendations.

The kingdom of Navarra encompassed parts of what is today known as the Basque Country, and you may hear Basque spoken. You will also see street signs in both Basque and Spanish. Bear in mind that parking in Pamplona, as in any large Spanish city, can be difficult.

PAMPLONA RECOMMENDED WINE SHOP

Museo del Vino Avenida Sancho El Fuerte (Antso Azkarra Etorbidea) 77, 31008 Pamplona/Iruña Tel: 948 279 877

Valle de Yerri, Navarra

(JESÚS CASO/ICEX)

Navarra's Wine Country

The wine country of Navarra begins almost immediately south of Pamplona. To head there, leave the city in the direction of Tudela, the province's second city. The town of Las Campanas, 15 km (9 miles) from Pamplona, is home to Vinícola Navarra, on the left-hand side of the road. Though the building may look old (dating back to 1850) it contains modern equipment. Much of the original building has been carefully restored, making this winery a good meta-phor for Navarra itself, a mixture of tradition and innovation.

Puente la Reina

On the other side of Las Campanas a turning to the west will lead you through hilly country dotted with vineyards and asparagus fields to Puente la Reina. For centuries this has been the junction of pilgrim routes that entered Spain through the passes of Somport and Roncesvalles. A statue of a pilgrim greets you at the entrance to the town.

The important winery

Señorío de Sarría, an estate complete with workers' village, and one of the region's most famous wine producers, lies on the outskirts. It is approached through a forest with occasional glimpses of the river and certainly justifies a visit.

Estella and Ayegui

A few kilometers south of Puente la Reina you will find Estella, also on the pilgrim route to Santiago. The fascinating architecture of this small town, built on both banks of the Ega River, includes the old palace of the Kings of Navarra. In the 19th century the palace became the headquarters of the Carlists, the supporters of Don Carlos de Borbón, Pretender to the Spanish throne.

Across the river in the neighboring town of Ayegui is the **monastery of Irache**, another picturesque stop on the pilgrim route. In the 16th century the monastery became a Benedictine university. Next door is **Bodegas Irache**, producer of highly regarded and popular wines. A visit to both is a rewarding experience.

Tafalla to Olite

The ancient town of Tafalla, immediately south of Pamplona, is worth a visit for its excellent restaurant, **Túbal**, owned and run by the

(MIGUEL ANGEL PÉREZ/ICEX)

The delicately carved Romanesque cloister at the church of San Pedro, Olite, Navarra

iconoclastic Atxen Jimenez.

If you are not yet hungry, take the road east out of town to Ujué, a picturesque town perched on a hillside with fabulous views, a fortress and a Romanesque church. Enjoy lunch or dinner at the highly recommended Restaurante **Mesón Las Torres**.

Fortified by your meal, you should then head south from Tafalla on the N-121 to Olite, the beating heart of Navarra's wine industry and the seat of EVENA, its highly rated enological station (center of wine studies). Overlooking the town is a great fortress with its massive ramparts and 15 towers originally built in the 16th century by Charles the Noble. Part of this monument has been converted into a comfortable Parador Nacional, making it an ideal overnight stop. Do not miss **Casa Zanito**, an excellent restaurant (with hotel).

Tudela, Cascante and Cintruénigo

For more history, take the N-121 south from Olite to a well-signposted turnoff east to the Cistercian monastery of La Oliva built in the 11th and 12th centuries. Otherwise continue south and then southeast to Tudela, a fascinating town with a splendid cathedral and several interesting palaces. The Hotel AC Tudela is well worth staying in.

Cascante is a short distance southwest along the N-121. This town has a fine basilica and parish church and is home to **Bodegas Guelbenzu**, one of the most dynamic wineries in Navarra. Guelbenzu makes some of the region's most interesting wines. The bodega occupies the basement and first floor of a house belonging to the family that owns it, and is surrounded by gardens bursting with flowers and trees. So visit the winery, have a tasting and then take a stroll around the grounds.

Some 20 minutes' drive to the west of Tudela is Cintruénigo. **Bodegas Julián Chivite** is a family-owned company on quite a different scale to the previous. Chivite wines have established a well-earned international reputation for quality. Do not be deceived by the size of the winery, quality is always to the fore here. It has a

Trout, Navarra style

(ANGEL ROBLEDO/ICEX)

cooperage to care for the barrels in its Aging Hall and modern fermentation equipment to ensure high-quality wine. A short walk away is the excellent **Restaurante Maher.**

BODEGAS & MORE

Cintruénigo is a mere 20-minute drive from Alfaro, the first town in the Rioja Baja. Alternatively, the N-232 leads to the Denomination of Campo de Borja in Aragón.

AYEGUI
Bodegas Irache SL Clle Monasterio de Irache, 1 31240 Ayegui By prior arrangement.

LAS CAMPANAS
Vinícola Navarra

Ctra Zaragoza Km 14 31398 Muruarte de Reta Tel: 948 360 131 Mon–Fri 9AM–2PM Closed Aug. Modern winery housed in 19th-century buildings.

CASCANTE
Bodegas Guelbenzu San Juan, 14, Cascante Tel: 948 850 055 (Ricardo Guelbenzu) info@guelbenzu.es www.guelbenzu.es Mon–Fri 9AM–2PM and 4PM–6PM Sat 9AM–2PM Gardens. Free tastings for groups by prior arrangement.

CINTRUÉNIGO
Bodegas Julián Chivite Calle Ribera, 34 31592 Cintruénigo Tel: 948 811 000

(Mercedes Chivite)
www.chivite.com
Mon–Fri 10AM–2PM
and 3PM–6PM
Closed Jul 15–Aug 18
By prior arrangement.

PUENTE LA REINA

Bodegas de Sarría Calle
Finca Señorío de Sarría s/n
31100 Puente la Reina
Tel: 948 202 200
info@bodesa.net
www.bodegadesarria.com
Mon–Fri 10AM–12 noon
Closed Jul–Oct.
English-speaking tours
sometimes available
through prior arrangement
(Telephone several days
before your visit.)

Food and festivals of Navarra

Virtually every town in
Navarra's wine country celebrates the end of *la vendimia*
(the harvest) in September
or October. Still, the one
fiesta beyond all others in
Navarra takes place in early
July in Pamplona. The city
literally explodes into an
almost unbelievable week
of mayhem, including run-
ning the bulls, drinking,
eating and dancing to celebrate the city's patron saint.

San Fermín is one of the
greatest and most exhilarat-
ing fiestas in Europe, if not
in the world. If you want to
take part, make sure that
you book your hotel room
well in advance, that you
have sensible footwear and
a white outfit with a red
bandana.

Navarra's cuisine

The great dishes of Nav-
arra are almost identical to
those of Rioja and Aragón.
Menestra de verduras and
chilindrón sauce for example,
can be found in all three
regions. In fact, the three
provinces are interrelated
in many ways, historically
and culturally, and it is
not surprising that their
regional cuisines bear a
family likeness.

The province has a
splendid range of raw
ingredients. Wild mush-
rooms grow in abundance,
mostly in the north, and
their sublime flavor can be
appreciated in the famous
Revuelto de setas where they
are combined with beaten
eggs and garlic. The north
also produces good trout
in its mountain streams.
Try these in the province's
most famous dish, *Trucha
a la Navarra*. Game birds

such as quail (*codornices*) and partridges (*perdices*) are prepared in a variety of ways, with vegetables, wine and even with bitter chocolate.

The southern part of the province, particularly the Ribera region on the banks of the Ebro, is famous for vegetables. Vegetable patches are a feature of the landscape, especially bright green clumps of asparagus fern. Artichokes and asparagus from the region are delicious, usually served as entrées with mayonnaise or vinaigrette.

This area is the home of some of the best peppers in the country, including *pimientos del piquillo*, so-called because of their beak-like shape. These are usually fried, to accompany grilled meat, stuffed with a variety of different ingredients, or made into the famous *chilindrón* sauce which accompanies two other very typical Navarra dishes, *Cordero* (roast lamb) or *Pimientos en Chilindrón*.

Food specialties

Bacalao al Ajoarriero There are many sophisticated variations to this traditional dish. It comes from the northern part of the region and used to be served to *arrieros* (muleteers) at roadside inns in the evening. The traditional version combines salt cod from the Basque coast with garlic, peppers and sometimes tomatoes and onions. In leading restaurants, shrimp, crayfish and even lobster are added.

Trucha a la Navarra Fried trout, often stuffed with ham and served with mushrooms, garlic and parsley.

Caldereta Ribereña As this is a peasant dish from the south of the province, the ingredients tend to vary. Basically, it is a stew made with whatever the cook has to hand.

Cordero en Chilindrón Although roast lamb is as popular in Navarra as it is throughout northern Spain, this is a typical and delicious alternative. The lamb is cooked with slices of ham and a sauce of garlic, onions, tomatoes and, of course, the famous red peppers. A variation is *Pimientos en Chilindrón* with large slices of peppers used instead of the lamb.

Perdiz a la Tudelana This dish is from the southern part of the province. Partridges are cooked with quartered apples and served with boiled potatoes and mushrooms.

WHERE TO STAY AND EAT

Cintruénigo

Restaurante Maher
Ribera, 19
31592 Cintruénigo
Tel: 948 811 150
www.hotelmaher.com

Olite

Casa Zanito
Calle Mayor, 16
31390 Olite
Tel: 948 740 087
contacto@casazanito.com
www.casazanito.com (H/R)

Parador Nacional
Príncipe de Viana
Plaza de Teobaldos, 2
31390 Olite
Tel: 948 740 000
www.parador.es (H)

Pamplona

Restaurante Hartza
Juan de Labrit, 19
31003 Pamplona
Tel: 948 224 568

Alhambra
Calle Bergamin, 7
31002 Pamplona
Tel: 948 245 007 (R)

Horno de Aralar
Calle San Nicolás, 12
31003 Pamplona
Tel: 948 221 116 (R)

Puente La Reina

Mesón del Peregrino
Carretera
N-111, Pamplona-Logroño
Km 23
31100 Puente La Reina
Tel: 948 340 075
elperegrino@terra.es
One of the most beautiful
restaurants of Navarra.

Tafalla

Restaurante Túbal
Plaza de Navarra, 4
31300 Tafalla
Tel: 948 700 852
www.restaurantetubal.com

Tudela

Hotel AC Ciudad
de Tudela
Calle Misericordia s/n
31500 Tudela
Tel: 948 402 440
www.ac-hotels.com

Ujué

Restaurante Mesón
Las Torres
Calle Santa Maria, 9
31496 Ujué
Tel: 948 739 052

RIOJA

T HE EMERGENCE OF OTHER top-class wine
regions in Spain may have tarnished Rioja's once
unquestioned crown as producer of the finest red
wine in the kingdom. However, the more you explore it
the greater the chance that you'll emerge admiring the
wines from this remarkable region. This is one of the
country's richest provinces thanks to its powerful agricultural sector, which produces some of the finest vegetables
in the country as well as world-famous wines. Eating and
drinking are taken seriously in Rioja and the hospitality of
its people is legendary.

The landscape is like a huge bowl, with the Sierra de
Cantabria as the northern lip, shielding the valley below
from the chill influence of the Bay of Biscay. For me, the
best way to approach Rioja is from the north, from
Vitoria/Gasteiz (place-names in the Basque Country are
often signposted in Spanish and/or Basque) using the
beautiful A-2124 road. After a slow rise through potato
fields and forests well stocked with wild boar you reach
the Puerto de Herrera and are suddenly confronted with
a magical landscape. Rioja, with its ancient little fortified
towns dotted east-to-west before you, perfectly reveals
its macroclimatic potential. Immediately below you is
Rioja Alavesa, the part under Basque government. To the
right is Rioja Alta and way in the distance is Rioja Baja.
All around you in this high altitude pass lie the brooding
mountains of the Sierra de Cantabria.

Touring in Rioja

The region's major roads, the N-232 and the A-68, flow
through the region from south-east to north-west like
vital arteries, making wine routes easy to work out.

**‹‹ A view through the vineyards of the once fortified town of Laguardia
in Rioja Alavesa**

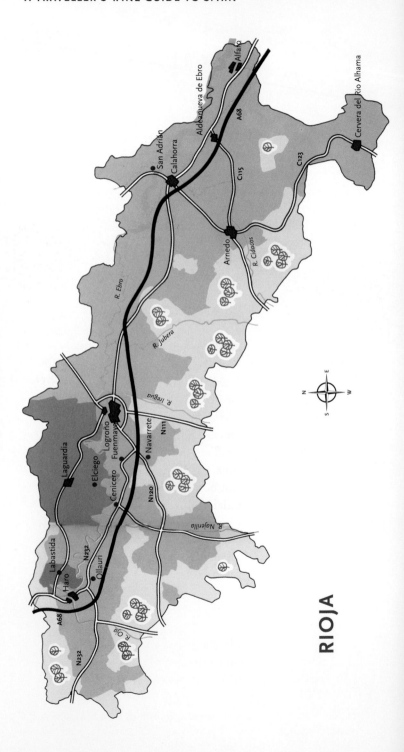

RIOJA

(HAROLD HECKLE)

Grapes of the rare Tempranillo peludo variety ripen in fall sunshine near San Vicente de la Sonsiera

With vineyards in three provinces —Rioja, Navarra and Alava—the wine region of the Rioja is divided into three zones: Rioja Alta to the west of Logroño; Rioja Alavesa to the north of the Ebro; and Rioja Baja, to the south and east.

Rioja Alta

Traditionally the home of Rioja's bigger wines, made from blends of the region's best grapes.

Rioja Alavesa

The region is where the Rioja revolution first began, this tends to be on higher ground, nearer the Cantabria mountain range. Because of the altitude, wines tend to be monovarietal, made from the early ripening Tempranillo.

Rioja Baja

The hottest part of Rioja is also in places some of the highest above sea level, giving a fascinating blend of warm country wine characteristics with delicate sophistication.

TO GET TO LOGROÑO

Logroño is 130 km (80 miles) south of Bilbao on the A-68; 350 km (217

miles) northeast of Madrid on the N-1 to Burgos, then the N-120, or 400 km (250 miles) via the N-1 to Burgos and the A-1 and A-68 (tolls).

Rioja— the grapes

Rioja covers some 63,500 hectares (157,150 acres) of vineyards. Since 1991 it has been granted the superior status of *Denominación de Origen Calificada*, equivalent to the Italian DOCG, the first such qualification in Spain. To achieve this status Rioja has demonstrated, over a long period, that its wines are consistently produced to the very highest standards.

Tempranillo is the leading grape of the region, followed by Garnacha and in lesser quantities Graciano and Mazuelo, which are usually planted in small parcels in the Alta. White wines are usually made

(BLANCA BERLIN/ICEX)

Bodega Ysios just outside Laguardia, designed by Santiago Calatrava; behind is the Sierra Cantabria mountain range

from Viura, though Malvasía and Garnacha Blanca are permitted.

Different soils and climates influence the type of grape varieties used in the three sub-regions. Hence, the red wines produced tend to differ in style. Baja, where the Garnacha predominates, tends to produce open, fruity wines with good color and higher alcohol. Alta tends to go for classic blends of Tempranillo, Garnacha, Mazuelo and Graciano, topped off with that unmistakeable oaky aroma so associated with Rioja.

Alavesa, where the Tempranillo is king, tends to produce leaner, less luscious wines but with more delicate aroma, greater elegance and a bit of acidity to help them improve during long periods of aging. Alavesa is famous for its young and fruity *joven* wines as well as its mature oak-aged blockbusters. Some wines are single-vineyard specialties, rare, expensive and wonderful. Other wines are specific to their sub-region, usually from Alta or Alavesa and a fair proportion are blends of wines from all three zones.

Rioja— The Bordeaux Legacy

The proximity between Rioja and Bordeaux has inevitably left the former with an important legacy, albeit mainly thanks to an American louse. The great French wine region

(JUAN MANUEL SANZ/ICEX)

is also largely responsible, if indirectly, for the two boom periods that shaped modern Rioja.

Rioja used to make wine in a similar fashion to most other Spanish regions, crushing the grapes and fermenting them in open stone *lagares*. Then, in the 1850-60s, a louse called phylloxera, which had inadvertently been introduced into France, attacked and laid waste to vast swathes of France's vineyards, forcing wine brokers and traders to seek alternative sources of wine.

Nearby Rioja offered enormous potential and was protected from infection (they thought) by the massive mountain chain of the Pyrenees. Many companies invested in Rioja and opened offices and even wineries, bringing with them valuable technical know-how.

Inevitably, phylloxera eventually spread to Spain. By then, however, Rioja had expanded and many of the methods of aging and production introduced by the French had taken root. Perhaps Bordeaux's greatest legacy is the use of destemmers and oak barrels. Wines were fermented in huge oak vats and, after a period of rest, pumped into classic Bordelaise barrels of 225 liters (roughly 50 gallons) where they were aged for years.

Oak aging is chiefly responsible for the distinctive vanilla-infused aroma of traditional Riojas. Whites deepen to an almost golden color and achieve a unique concentration of fruit, flavor and acidity. The reds lighten to a sultry tawny color with a wonderful balance between fruit and oakiness. All have a distinctive soft vanilla presence that has been the region's hallmark.

The 1970s boom

In the 1970s Rioja experienced another revolution with far-reaching consequences, and again Bordeaux was the catalyst. Claret prices had risen exorbitantly, and wine merchants were once more looking to other regions. They re-discovered Rioja, where some wine was still

« Oak barriques age wine gently in the old stone winery of Marqués de Riscal in Elciego

(HAROLD HECKLE)

Bodegas Bilbaínas, maker of Viña Pomal wine, in Haro

being made with methods imported from Bordeaux. The region was dragged into the international limelight and demand rose, triggering an inward flow of investment.

With investment came new technology, such as the hygiene that stainless steel offered. Stainless steel was initially used in milk and cheese production and rapidly adapted to winemaking, where it worked near miracles in terms of the purity of the fruit. These changes were most immediately felt in formerly rough-and-ready white and *rosado* wines. With hygiene came temperature-controlled fermentations that conveyed new dimensions in freshness and aroma. Young Rioja wines suddenly became a palatable reality.

Red wines became subtler in flavor. Instead of aging reds for very long periods in barrel, and then bottling and releasing them six months later, they began to be aged for less time in barrel and longer in bottle. The result was less oaky but perhaps much more complex and elegant wines.

FOR FURTHER INFORMATION
The Consejo Regulador has an excellent website for in-depth consultation: Calle Estambrera, 52, 26006 Logroño. Tel: 941 500 400 info@riojawine.com www.riojawine.com

Rioja Baja
Rioja Baja is the warmest and most southerly of the region's three sub-zones, a flat plain of ochre-colored fields lying alongside the great Ebro river, inter-

spersed with some higher semi-mountainous land. Few bodegas of note have made a base here so it is off the track usually beaten by wine buffs. But don't let this stop you from exploring! Garnacha is dominant here and can produce some luscious wines with color, body and considerable liveliness.

Alfaro

Alfaro is a small agricultural town featuring the Hotel Palacios. There is a wine and fossil museum and an excellent restaurant. It is next to the much-improved **Bodegas Palacio Remondo**, famed for belonging to the family of Alvaro Palacios, one of Spain's iconic winemakers. Nearby there is also one of the best restaurants of the Rioja Baja, the **Asador San Roque**, which offers good regional food with excellent vegetable dishes. In short, a good overnight stop.

Calahorra

This was once a Roman city and today acts as a large and busy commercial hub for the local agricultural community. The town has several good restaurants and one of the region's two Paradors. The road west to Arnedo (LR-115) takes you along the pretty Cidacos River to the small town of Quel, home of Bodegas Ontañón.

From Calahorra it is about 50 km (30 miles) to Logroño either along the N-232 or the A-68 toll *autopista*. Both roads go through the heart of Rioja to Haro and the Basque country beyond.

Grávalos and Arnedillo

The LR-123 to Grávalos takes you to the small, family-owned **Bodegas Escudero** where some of the most exciting Garnacha of the region can be tasted, if you're lucky. This ever-busy family even produces a sparkling wine made from Chardonnay grown in its own vineyards.

Ask for directions at either bodega to the nearby site where dinosaur footprints have been found. Just before Arnedillo you come to the **Molino del Cidacos**, a small hotel, restaurant and winery, all housed in an old converted windmill.

GRÁVALOS

Bodegas Escudero
Ctra de Amedo, 26587
Grávalos.
Tel: 941 398 008
info@bodegasescudero.com
www.bodegasescudero.com

QUEL

Bodegas Ontañón
Avda de Aragón, 3
26006 Logroño
Tel: 690 858 519
enoturismo@ontanon.es
www.ontanon.es
Collection of sculptures
and paintings.

Logroño

Logroño is a prosperous
and orderly provincial
city. Locals enjoy going
out *de tapeo* (trying tapas in
different establishments).
Calle de los Laureles near
the central square is a great
place to start. Logroño is
also a real wine city. Famous
labels stare out at you from
bottles in the windows of
grocery and wine shops,
while the wine lists of its
restaurants seem to burst
with local pride, displaying
what almost amounts to a
roll of honor of the Spanish
wine industry.

Logroño is home to
several leading bodegas.
Around 3 km (2 miles)
from the city center on the
southbound N-232 is the
famous **Bodegas Marqués
de Murrieta**. Founded in
1848, it claims to be the
oldest wine company in
the Rioja. Now owned by
Vicente Cebrián, Count of
Creixell, a nobleman from
Galicia, the winery is a
must for any wine visitor.
Entrance to the winery is
tricky, as it is only ap-
proachable via the west-
bound lane of the N-232.

Closer to the city center
on the west bank of Ebro
River is another historic
company, **Bodegas Franco-
Españolas**, founded in
1901 by a Frenchman flee-
ing phylloxera. The whole
complex, with its extensive
underground cellars, is
lovingly maintained.

Bodegas Olarra was built
during the 1970s boom
by a steel magnate. As such it
represents the second phase
of modernization in Rioja.
It was modelled on the wineries of California and built
in the shape of a Y to repre-
sent the three sub-zones of
Rioja. It produces a wide
range of wine styles including a bubbly, all of which
are for sale in the shop.

The tiny hamlet of Oyón (Oion) a few kilometers north of Logroño is home to the family-owned **Bodegas Martínez Bujanda.** This is a modern, high-tech winery that, under the guidance of the Martínez Bujanda brothers, particularly the energetic Carlos, produces a superb range of wines. The family also owns a single vineyard estate called Finca Valpiedra. Ask to visit that superb property.

If you continue on the A-3226 past Oyón you'll come to another tiny village, Moreda, wedged deep within a valley. The tiny Moreda River provides this corner of Alavesa with its own microclimate, which **Bodegas Fernández de Piérola** exploits with great elegance. The winery is perched up on the high ground above the village and provides excellent views of the dry stone terracing of Alavesa. Try the delicate, barrique-fermented white as well as the blockbuster Vitium Reserva.

A worthwhile detour leads you to the ancient Chabola de la Hechicera dolmen. To get there turn north on the A-124 at Assa and head for Lanciego.

BODEGAS & MORE

LOGROÑO
Bodegas Marqués de Murrieta
Finca Ygay
Ctra Logroño-Zaragoza
Km 5, 26006 Logroño
Tel: 941 271 370
rrpp@marquesdemurrieta.com
www.marquesdemurrieta.com

Bodegas Olarra SA
Polígono de Cantabria s/n
26004 Logroño
Tel: 941 235 299
bodegasolarra@bodegasolarra.es
www.bodegasolarra.es

(HAROLD HECKLE)

Very old Garnacha vines southeast of Rioja

OYÓN
Bodegas Martínez Bujanda
Camino Viejo s/n
01320 Oyón
Tel: 941 622 188
bujanda@bujanda.com
(Carlos Martínez Bujanda)

Rioja Alta and Alavesa

The N-232 is busy east of Logroño and even busier to the west. Still, this route is a good way to see the countryside of the Rioja Alta and Alavesa, with glimpses of vineyards and good views of the river and the Sierra beyond. Perhaps even better is the A-124, especially if you choose to make Laguardia your base—as good a plan as any.

A central church and the Casa Real, a crumbling stately home, dominate Fuenmayor in Rioja Alta. All around the central square are bars, which, just before the start of the harvest, are packed with workers waiting for the

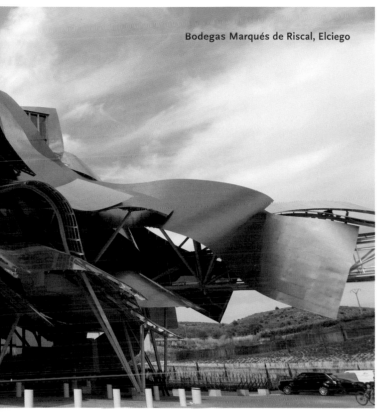

Bodegas Marqués de Riscal, Elciego

(JUAN MANUEL SANZ/ICEX)

picking to begin. Saturday night transforms the town, like in so much of Rioja, when these bars fill with cheerful grape farmers and winemakers coming into town for a glass or two.

Rioja Alavesa is part of the Basque country in the province of Alava. Laguardia is at the heart of Alavesa, where Tempranillo is king. It is said that a discerning palate can identify Alavesa wines from their Alta brothers for their elegance and Tempranillo-led structure, as opposed to the bigger wines of Alta.

Laguardia

Laguardia stands against the magnificent backdrop of the Sierra Cantabria. From here you can plan visits to some of Spain's most remarkable wineries. One is **Bodegas Ysios**, a stunning architectural tour de force by renowned architect Santiago Calatrava. The second, which from the outside looks somewhat

(ICEX)

The barrel hall at Bodegas Ysios, near Laguardia, designed by Valencia-born architect Santiago Calatrava

like a flying saucer perched on a hillside and from the inside like a set from a James Bond film, is CVNE (Compañía Vitivinícola del Norte de España). Around the other side of the hill is **Bodegas Contino**, one of Rioja's most attractive single-vineyard estate wineries. La Granja Nuestra Señora de Remelluri, which is further up into the mountains, is another quality-conscious firm.

Elciego

Follow the A-3210 south from Laguardia and you come to the lovely town of Elciego. For wine historians and architecture fans, this is a place of pilgrimage. Elciego is the location of the famous and historic winery of **Marqués de Riscal**, enriched by its wild hotel designed by Frank O Gehry. This was the first winery in the region to be built along

French lines, with essential information smuggled in by Jean Pineau, in 1858. Pineau had been paid handsomely to leave Bordeaux and bring his knowledge to Rioja in a scandal that was almost Cold War-like in its intrigue.

Pineau had worked for 20 years as winemaker at Château Lanessan. Keen to copy Bordeaux's success, Camilo Hurtado de Amézaga, Marquis of Riscal, approached Pineau and commissioned the design of a winery modelled on those of Bordeaux. The resulting bodega, built of soft sandstone in the middle of its vineyards, still stands as a testimony to the French contribution to Rioja's wine industry.

Cenicero

From Elciego it is a 15-minute drive on the N-232, a scenic road, to Cenicero in Rioja Alta. One in every three hectares here are planted with vines and, in good years, the town and its two neighbors, Huércanos and Uruñuela, produce more than 20 million liters (about 5 million gallons) of high-quality wine. Every year during the first week of September Cenicero embarks on ten days of eating, drinking and celebrating its patron saint, Santa Daría. On the final day there is the ritual pressing of the first wine of the year. However, some of the town's many bodegas shut down for the duration, so avoid this week if winery visits are your main concern.

Bodegas Riojanas lies on the town's main road near the railway line and was built in 1890 by French technicians. Wines like Monte Real bear the name of single vineyards.

Just around the corner on the eastern approach to the town is another of Cenicero's most influential bodegas, **Marqués de Cáceres**. French influence comes through the Franco-Spanish Forner family, who also own Château Camensac in Bordeaux. In the early 1970s, the winery became one of the region's great innovators, introducing careful temperature-controlled fermentation methods to extract maximum freshness and aroma from white wines and Bordeaux-like oak aging for the reds. Revolutionary at the time, these methods have now been imitated by many regional companies.

Briones

On the N-232 between Ce-
nicero and Haro you'll find
Briones, one of the prettiest
towns in Rioja. What makes
a visit here an absolute must
is that it contains one of the
best wine museums in the
world. The Museo Dinastía
Vivanco illustrates and
explains the history of wine
using some of the most
fascinating exhibits dedicated to the subject. The
admirable collection housed
within features priceless
pieces from the dawn of
winemaking through to the
present day, including paintings by Picasso and beautiful Greek craters. As part of
the museum there is a good
restaurant with spectacular
views across endless vineyards as well as the adjacent
and impressive Bodega

Dinastía Vivanco.

While in Briones it is well
worth paying a visit to the
small, artisinal and homely
Bodegas Miguel Merino.

BODEGAS & MORE

BRIONES

Museo Dinastía Vivanco
Carretera Nacional, 232
26330 Briones
Tel: 902 320 001
infomuseo@dinastiavivanco.es
www.dinastiavivanco.com

Bodegas Miguel Merino
Carretera de Logroño, 16
26330 Briones
Tel: 941 322 263
info@miguelmerino.com
www.miguelmerino.com

CENICERO
Bodegas Riojanas
Carretera de la Estación 1-21

Old bush Tempranillo vines in winter, Rioja

(HAROLD HECKLE)

26350 Cenicero
Tel: 941 454 050
info@bodegasriojanas.com
www.bodegasriojanas.com

Unión-Viti-Vinícola
Bodegas Marqués de
Cáceres Ctra de Logroño
s/n, 26350 Cenicero
Tel: 941 455 064
www.marquesdecaceres.com

ELCIEGO
Marqués de Riscal
Calle Torrea 1
01340 Elciego
Tel: 945 606 000
marquesderiscal@
marquesderiscal.com
www.marquesderiscal.com

LAGUARDIA
Bodegas Ysios
Camino de La Hoya s/n
01300 Laguardia
Tel: 945 600 640
ysios@domecqbodegas.com
www.bodegasysios.com

CVNE (Compañía
Vitivinícola del Norte de
España) Bodega Viña Real
Ctra Logroño-Laguardia
Km 4.8, 01300 Laguardia
Tel: 945 625 255
visitas@cvne.com
www.cvne.com

La Granja Nuestra
Señora de Remelluri
Ctra Rivas de Tereso s/n

01300 Laguardia
Tel: 945 331 801
(Vega González)
www.remelluri.com

Viñedos del Contino
Ctra Logroño-Laguardia
Km. 4.8, 01300 Laguardia
Tel: 945 625 255
marketing@cvne.com
www.cvne.com
Note that the address on
the website does not match
this. That's because you
can't simply drive up to the
winery. You have to go via
Cune. Contino is a farm
within the larger Cune
estate.

Haro

From Cenicero the N-232
rises steadily to the town
of Haro. Some 2 km (over
a mile) from the first exit,
there is a turn-off to the
south that leads to the
quiet hamlet of Ollauri.
If you can arrange a visit
to the **Paternina Winery**,
this could be a highlight of
a tour of Rioja. Federico
Paternina is one of the
largest wine companies of
the region with a modern
complex on the outskirts
of Haro. Its deep under-
ground cellars at Ollauri,
dug by Portuguese workers
during the 16th century, are

one of the Rioja's show-pieces. There is something almost frightening about them, with their long, low corridors, their blackened, musty, dripping walls and their bins of old bottles.

Further up the road you come to the elegant, pros-perous town of Haro, the proud beating heart of Rioja Alta. Haro has one of the leading enological stations in Spain, a wine museum, several wine companies and fine restaurants. If you ap-proach via the N-232, take the second exit, which leaves the road in a broad arc to the right and then crosses over a bridge. This leads to the **Barrio de La Estación** quarter around the railway station, the area with the greatest concentration of bodegas. Many of these are prestigious, with ancient traditions.

First, there is the taste-fully modernized but tradi-tional and highly respected La Rioja Alta. Across the road is **López de Heredia** with its modern-style tower. This firm prides itself on an unbroken adherence to traditional methods of fermentation (in oak vats), production and aging, and whose winery (including a cooperage) is virtually

a working museum. The Rioja Alta section of CVNE (Compañía Vinícola del Norte de España) is located here and produces high quality wines such as Impe-rial (as opposed to Alavesa's Viña Real).

Bodegas Bilbaínas, now in the hands of the Raventós dynasty (based on Cava wealth) has the most extensive underground cel-lars in the Rioja. Its wines have improved dramatically in recent years. The large **Bodegas Muga** has a win-ery, housed in lovely old sandstone buildings, which is almost a monument to the oak barrel and the vat. Visits to these companies, regarded as real aristocrats in Rioja, will be a reward-ing experience.

Haro is a great town to wander around in and it is a good place to stay overnight. It has a pleasant central square surrounded by ar-cades and old houses dating back to the 18th century. Very comfortable accom-modation can be found at the historic Los Agostinos hotel, Hostal Iturrimuri on the N-232 or the Parador at Santo Domingo de la Calzada, some 15 minutes' drive out of town.

The town offers a feast of

tapas and more substantial dishes. The famous **Mesón Terete** in the center is a good place to start a tour. Specializing in lamb roasted in a baker's oven, and served at simple wooden tables, it is a must for all travellers in the Rioja.

BODEGAS & MORE

Haro city website:
www.haro.org

Federico Paternina, SA
Avda Santo Domingo, 11
26200 Haro
Tel: 941 310 550
www.paternina.com
Apply here to visit the cellars in Ollauri.

Bodegas Muga
Barrio de la Estación s/n
26200 Haro
Tel: 941 311 825
info@bodegasmuga.com
www.bodegasmuga.es

R López de Heredia Viña Tondonia SA
Avda de Vizcaya, 3
26200 Haro
Tel: 941 310 244
bodega@lopezdeheredia.com
www.lopezdeheredia.com

Companía Vinícola del Norte de España (CVNE)
Barrio de la Estación s/n
26200 Haro
Tel: 941 304 800
marketing@cvne.com
www.cvne.com

La Rioja Alta SA Avda de Vizcaya, 8, 26200 Haro. Tel: 941 310 346. (Marta Enciso) riojalta@riojalta.com www.riojalta.com Visit also sister company **Torre de Oña** in Laguardia.

Food and festivals of Rioja

Rioja's cuisine is based on the sheer quality of its raw materials. Fresh fish is brought from the Basque coast. Lamb and wild boar are reared or hunted in the hills above Alta and Alavesa. Baja is one of the great gardens of Spain, producing excellent vegetables: artichokes, asparagus, tomatoes, lettuce and peppers. Lamb, as in much of Spain, occupies a central position in the local cuisine. Dishes range from the classic *Cordero lechal asado* (roast milk-fed lamb) to lamb chops grilled over a fire of vine prunings, another regional favorite. The local *chorizo*, not as spicy as some in Spain,

(HAROLD HECKLE)

An al fresco lunch is prepared to accompany a tasting at Bodegas La Emperatriz, Baños de Rioja

adds bite to stews such as *Patatas a la Riojana*.

Asparagus is an important element of the region's cuisine. Peppers, preferably the famous *pimientos del piquillo*, make an appearance in most local meals, be they stewed, baked or fried, served alongside meat, or stuffed. An unforgettable vegetable dish is *Menestra de Verduras*, which shows off local produce at its very best.

Wine festivals

Every town in the Rioja has a patron saint's day, which is celebrated with a public holiday when the bars and streets fill till the early hours of the morning.

Feasts to remember are **Santa Daría** in Cenicero (early September), and the two main festivals of Haro and Logroño.

The Wine Battle or Batalla del Vino on St

Peter's Day, June 29, in Haro is an absolutely savage affair. A Bacchanalian feast in the truest of senses, festivities start with a march around the city. Next, participants (including many unsuspecting foreigners) walk to a chapel on the hillside of San Felices, some 3 km (2 miles) from Haro. It is there that the battlers, traditionally dressed in white, pour industrial quantities of wine on each other before having breakfast next to open fires. Then everyone returns on foot to Haro, literally drenched in wine.

The Feria de San Mateo in Logroño on St Matthew's Day, September 21, is a more sedate affair. Traditionally it was supposed to mark the beginning of the harvest. There is a serious religious aspect to the festival, but there is plenty of jollity and drinking to accompany it.

Food specialties

Callos a La Riojana Tripe cooked with whole chorizos, ham, nuts and several different vegetables and spices.

Chuleta de Ternera a la Riojana A typical dish, it combines grilled meat such as veal chops sprinkled with chopped garlic, parsley and peppers.

Menestra de Verduras A local favorite which combines the region's wonderful vegetables, artichokes, peas and asparagus, with cured ham and eggs which are either hard boiled or beaten into the mixture.

Cordero asado Baby (28 days old) lamb baked in an earthenware dish and served with a salad. Try baby lettuce split in half and mixed with vinaigrette, garlic and anchovies.

Patatas a la Riojana A simple, hearty potato stew cooked with chorizo, garlic, onion and a little white wine.

Pimientos rellenos de Codornices Peppers stuffed with quails.

Solomillo al vino de Rioja A delicious dish where wine is used copiously. Beefsteaks are macerated in red wine and brandy and are cooked with mushrooms and small onions.

WHERE TO STAY AND EAT

Alfaro

Hotel Palacios
Ctra Zaragoza, 6
Exit no. 16 on the A-68
motorway
26540 Alfaro
Tel: 941 180 100
palacios@villacastejon.com
Ask here to visit Bodega
Palacio Remondo next
door.

Asador San Roque
Calle San Roque, 3
26540 Alfaro
Tel: 941 182 888
www.asadorsanroque.com (R)

Arnedillo

El Molino del Cidacos
Ctra Arnendo, Km. 14
26589 La Rioja
Tel: 941 394 063
elmolino@pegarrido.com
www.pegarrido.com (H/R)
Good wine shop attached.

Calahorra

Parador
Plaza Mercadal
26500 Calahorra
Tel: 941 130 358
www.parador.es

Casa Mateo
Plaza El Raso 15
26500 Calahorra
Tel: 941 130 009 (R)

Haro

Los Agustinos
San Agustín 2
26200 Haro
Tel: 941 311 308
losagostinos@aranzauzu-
hoteles.com
www.hotellosagustinos.com
Housed in a charming
14th-century convent (H)

**Parador at Santo Domingo
de la Calzada**
Plaza del Santo, 3
26250 Santo Domingo
de la Calzada
Tel: 941 340 300
www.parador.es

Mesón Terete
Calle Lucrecia Arana, 17
26200 Haro.
Tel: 941 310 023 (R)

Beethoven I
Santo Tomás, 8
26200 Haro
Tel: 941 310 018 (R)

Beethoven II
Santo Tomás, 3-5
26200 Haro
Tel: 941 311 181 (R)

Beethoven III
Plaza de la Iglesia, 8
26200 Haro
Tel: 941 303 887
All Beethovens are run by
the same management.

(HAROLD HECKLE)

Workers at Bodegas La Emperatriz in Rioja light dry vine cuttings for use in an aromatic barbecue

The first is an elegant restaurant, the second and third are more relaxed *mesónes*. Good regional food.

Atamauri
Plaza Juan García Gato, 1
26200 Haro
Tel: 941 303 220
Great tapas.

Logroño

Cachetero
Calle Laurel, 3
26001 Logroño
Tel: 941 228 463
Very good food.
Expensive.

Las Cubanas
San Agustín, 17
26001 Logroño
Tel: 941 220 050
Good Rioja cuisine.

Restaurante Iruña
Calle Laurel, 8
26001 Logroño
Tel: 941 220 064
Traditional.

ARAGÓN

THE ANCIENT KINGDOM OF ARAGÓN, which lies between Catalonia to the east and the great vineyards of Rioja and Navarra to the west, has in recent years experienced a radical re-think on how wine should be made. An industry that dates back to the third century BC has been turned into one of the most modern and dynamic in Spain.

Somontano

This region of Aragón has a long history of winemaking and has been the natural home of one of Europe's great red varieties, Garnacha. Located in Alto or high Aragón, in the lee of the Pyrenees, the name Somontano literally means "beside the mountains." The region has carved a niche for itself by planting imported grapes such as Chardonnay, Gewürztraminer and Cabernet Sauvignon. While ancestral Moristel and Parraleta are still grown in small quantities, they have made way for, or in some cases been blended into, ultra-modern styles that have become popular in Spain.

The DO was established in 1984. When planning your trip, your first and most important port of call should be its headquarters, where you will find the offices of *Ruta del Vino Somontano* (the region's wine routes). Natalia Gracia Malo will be happy to plan a tailor-made trip for you. Even if you have no idea where you want to go, she will prepare a route for you—an invaluable service to wine tourists.

Though the odd gem can be found elsewhere in Aragón, wine lovers should head straight to Barbastro, in the northern region of Huesca. To get there take the E-804 from Logroño to Zaragoza, then the E-7 to Huesca and finally the A-22 to Barbastro. You can also take the bullet train from Madrid or Barcelona to Zaragoza and

« The collegiate Church of Santa María, part of a monastery, tops a rocky bluff at Alquézar, Somontano

ARAGÓN

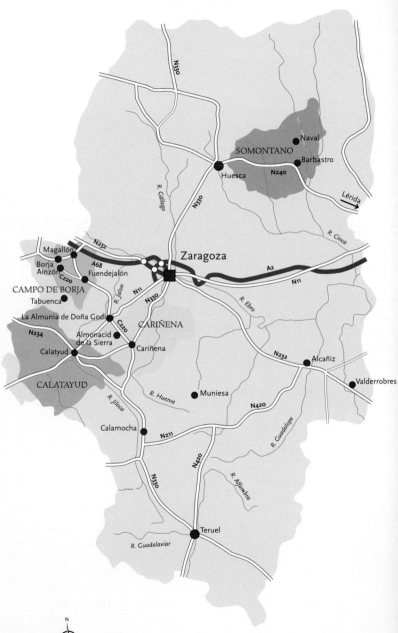

rent a car from there.

Zaragoza, the ancient capital of Aragón, is well worth exploring. Notable highlights include its ancient Moorish fort, called Aljafería, and its cathedral, La Seo. Note that the cathedral is not the largest religious building in Zaragoza—that distinction goes to the rather dull Pilar church.

In Barbastro, terraces on Paseo del Coso afford visitors an opportunity to enjoy a drink, tapas and dinner among local residents on a lovely tree-lined avenue. If you don't fancy the relative bustle of downtown Barbastro, the ancient medieval stone village of Alquézar is a stunning rural alternative. With its fort (now a monastery) overlooking the hilltop town and the steep Vero Valley below, it exudes character. Walkers, rafters and rowers love the area for its variety of water sports within its steep valleys.

FOR FURTHER INFORMATION
Denominación de Origen Somontano
Avenida de la Merced, 64
22300 Barbastro
Tel: 974 315 575
somontano@dosomontano.com
www.dosomontano.com

Ruta del Vino Somontano
Avenida de la Merced, 64
22300 Barbastro
Tel: 974 316 509
info@rutadelvinosomontano.com
rutadelvinosomontano.com

The history of the region is linked to the cooperative, now called Bodegas Pirineos. The co-op was established in 1964 with 200 members. Today most are still there, including the Subidos family, which has four generations working in grape and wine production. The co-op provides the winery with 1000 hectares, though today Barbadillo, of sherry fame, has bought many shares, turning the enterprise into a company. Montesierra is Pirineos' main label but you should also try Mesache and Pirineos. Marboré is the top range, with a blend of Tempranillo, Merlot, Cabernet Sauvignon, Moristel and Parraleta that is very good.

Viñas del Vero, established in 1986, is a large winery and controls 1160 hectares, of which 750 are wholly owned. Plantations were made after a study with UC Davis in California to determine which varieties were best suited

(HAROLD HECKLE)

Very old Garnacha bush vines are slow to awaken in spring at Bodegas Niño Jesús, near Aniñón, Calatayud

to the region. The winery is currently owned by the Gonzalez Byass group (since 2008). Their top wine is Secastilla although they also own Blecua, a separate 11-hectare estate which makes its blockbuster wines. All their wines, from a distinctive Gewürztraminer to Gran Vos Reserva (Cabernet and Merlot second-year wood) are superbly made and excellent value. Blecua, usually a Cabernet, Merlot, Garnacha and Tempranillo blend, often exhibits a huge nose, beautiful maturity with freshness and lots of tannins.

For those looking for a view into an achingly beautiful yet almost antiquely traditional winery, **Bodegas Lalanne** is a must. Currently run by sisters Leonor, Lucrecia and Laura Lalanne, whose family arrived from France in 1842 to escape the phylloxera. Different branches of the family have wineries in Argentina and Bordeaux. They make a Gewürztraminer–Chardonnay that is exotic and clean. Some of their reds, however, are closer to the 19th century than the 21st.

Those interested in more daring design should visit **Bodegas Laus**. Property developer Luis Zozaya built this architectural *tour de force* with a three-million-liter capacity. His idea is to eventually have a hotel and health spa attached. For the moment the wines are testament to modernity and value for money. From their Flor de Chardonnay, through their Laus tinto Roble (Merlot, Cabernet and Tempranillo—five months in oak) to their Reservas, you will be enthralled. **Bodegas Irius,** exactly opposite Laus, is another architectural masterpiece.

A little north of Barbastro, in the town of Salas Bajas, lies **Enate, Viñedos y Crianzas del Alto Aragón.** Founded in 1991, the first vintage was in 1992 from the winery's own 500 hectares. The Nozaleda family, which owns most of the shares, made their fortune in America and 25 years ago became involved in Spanish real estate before investing in wine. Jesús Sesé was a vineyard owner who exchanged his land to become a shareholder in this 3.5-million-bottle (4000-barrel) capacity venture. You should try Enate's utterly modern Chardonnay (both young and barrique fermented) as well as their Merlot and Cabernet Sauvignon blends. Enate makes a top white called Enate Uno (so far 2003 and 2006 vintages only), which is an expensive eye-opener.

BODEGAS & MORE

BARBASTRO

Bodegas Pirineos Crta Barbastro-Nava Km 3.5 Barbastro. Tel: 974 311 289

Viñas del Vero
Crta de Naval, Km 3.7
22300 Barbastro
Tel: 974 302 216
info@Viñasdelvero.es
www.Viñasdlvero.es

Bodegas Lalanne
Castillo San Marcos, s/n
22300 Barbastro
Tel: 974 310 689
lalanne@bodegaslalanne.com

Bodegas Laus, SL
Ctra Nacional 240 Km
154.8, 22300 Barbastro
Tel: 974 269 708
www.bodegaslaus.com

Bodegas Irius
Opposite Laus is another architectural masterpiece.
Tel: 902 122 211
marketing@bodegairius.com
www.bodegairius.com

HUESCA

**Enate, Viñedos y
Crianzas del Alto Aragón**
Avda de las Artes, 1
22314 Salas Bajas
Tel: 974 302 580
bodega@enate.es

Other wines and wine villages of Aragón

Campo de Borja, the most westerly of Aragón's DOs, is rich in wine culture, with towns like Fuendejalón, Magallón, Borja, Ainzón and Tabuenca, which have for decades been suppliers of pleasantly fruity bulk wine to Spain and further afield. Cariñena is known for its soft, slightly jammy wines.

(HAROLD HECKLE)

The modern architecture of Bodegas Laus, Barbastro, Somontano; a new hotel/spa is being planned here

WHERE TO STAY AND EAT

Barbastro

La Bodega del Vero
Calle Romero, 13
22300 Barbastro
Tel: 974 311 183
This is an old chocolate
factory with beautiful
cellars. Upstairs is a good
shop while the restaurant
is underground.

Flor
Calle Goya, 3
Tel: 974 311 056
flor@restauranteflor.com
www.restauranteflor.com
Traditional fare served
with flair.

**Gran Hotel
"Ciudad de Barbastro"**
Plaza del Mercado, 4
22300 Barbastro
Tel: 974 308 900
www.ghbarbastro.com
A comfortable establish-
ment facing the city's
pleasant market square.

Alquézar

Hotel Maribel
Calle Arrabal s/n
22145 Alquézar
Tel: 974 318 979
hotelmaribel@torra.es
An exclusive, beautiful
stone town palace. For
alternatives check:
www.alquezar.org

The entrance to
Bodegas Irius,
Barbastro

NORTHEAST
SPAIN

WINE CULTURE PROBABLY ENTERED the Spanish mainland through the Ebro River delta between two and three thousand years ago. Hence this northeastern corner of the peninsula, looking out over the Mediterranean, has some of the deepest enological roots of western Europe.

Catalonia

Catalonia, as the region is known today, was once part of an ancient kingdom that straddled the Pyrenees. It has its own language, proud cultural heritage and strong national identity. Its origins go back to Charlemagne's creation of a *Marca Hispanica* in 795 AD. This was a group of early Iberian counties and lordships, of which Andorra is the sole autonomous survivor. In 1137 the area which today encompasses Catalonia became the Kingdom of Aragón.

Linked to early seafaring traders, Catalans have inherited a good business sense. A local saying, *la pela es la pela* (money is money) captures this concept well, as does the notion that Catalans count even when they dance their ancestral and precise *sardana*. The standard of living here, based on manufacturing and commerce, has historically been the highest in the country, along with that in the industrial Basque region. To some extent, agriculture played a subsidiary part in this boom during much of the 20th century.

The exception is the wine industry, which has flourished during two quite specific periods. The first came as a response to the phylloxera infestation that hit France in the 1860s. Catalan businessmen stepped in quickly, converting much of the countryside to viticulture to supply

≪ The 14th-century Perelada Castle, illuminated against the evening sky in Girona, contains a wine museum and fine cellar

NORTHEAST SPAIN

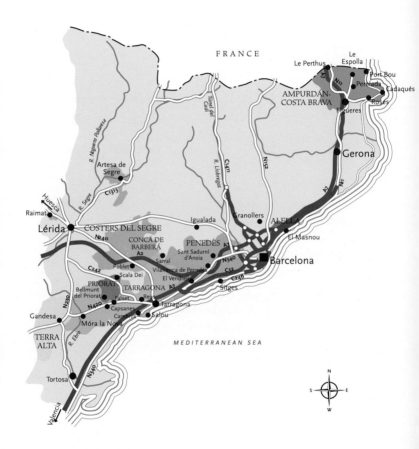

FRANCE

Le Perthus

Le Espolla

Port Bou

AMPURDÁN-
COSTA BRAVA

Perelada

Cadaqués

Roses

Figueres

Gerona

Tunel del Cadí

R. Noguera Pallaresa

R. Segre

Artesa de Segre

C1313

R. Segre

C1411

R. Llobregat

N152

Huesca

Raimat

Lérida

N240

COSTERS DEL SEGRE

Igualada

Granollers

ALELLA

El Masnou

CONCA DE
BARBERÁ

PENEDÈS

A2

Sarral

Sant Sadurní
d'Anoia

N340

Barcelona

C242

Poblet

Scala Dei

Vilafranca de Penedès

El Vendrell

C32

C246

Sitges

PRIORAT

TARRAGONA

Bellmunt
del Priorat

Falset

Reus

N420

Capsanes

Tarragona

N330

Gandesa

Móra la Nova

Cambrils

Salou

TERRA
ALTA

R. Ebro

MEDITERRANEAN SEA

N340

Tortosa

Valencia

N S E W

Boquería Market, Barcelona

(HAROLD HECKLE)

thirsty French markets that had been left without home-produced wine. This period of bounty was followed by a catastrophic collapse when phylloxera jumped across the Pyrenees and devastated Catalan vineyards, causing unimaginable hardship to the point of starvation in some areas. The second golden period came with the post-phylloxera development of the Cava industry, which provided fresh hope in once hard-hit rural areas and spurred a general renaissance.

Barcelona

Set between verdant mountains and the Mediterranean Sea, the Catalan capital basks in a well-earned reputation as one of Europe's most popular destinations. With a dramatic rocky coastline cradling little fishing ports to the north and almost endless sandy beaches stretching to the south, Barcelona has acted as a powerful tourist magnet since the late 1950s. Around 60 million foreign visitors a year make Spain the world's third most visited holiday destination. Thanks to its setting, the beauty of Catalonia, its coasts and offshore islands, not to mention its food and wine, millions explore Barcelona annually. Once there it is easy to understand why.

Rising majestically behind the city is the Tibidabo, an imposing pine-covered mountain that frames the metropolis, its urban sprawl and vast port beside a glittering sea. *Tibi dabo* is Latin for "I give thee," which according to the gospels of Luke and Matthew is what the devil said, offering Christ the glories of the world were he but to kneel and worship him. Barcelona, nestled beneath the Tibidabo, truly encompasses all known earthly pleasures.

The city is compact and exceptionally pedestrian-friendly, hence using a car is unnecessary until you decide to venture to the surrounding wine regions. It is sensible to buy a 10-trip card from any metro railway station. This entitles you to take city buses as well as underground trains and works out at about a dollar a trip. However, you do not need to travel to the outskirts to find accommodation and food. Hotels and inexpensive hostels in the Ciutat Vella, the Gothic quarter deep in the heart of the city and locally referred to as **Barri Gòtic**, are reasonably priced and ideally situated.

La Rambla is a pedestrian street of about three-quarters of a mile that runs through the city center, and the best breakfast in Barcelona is to be found in **La Boqueria**, Barcelona's central market just west of La Rambla, near the port. One market stall there has some of the best fruit juices available anywhere in Spain and prices are reasonable.

Modern architecture in a barrel hall in the DO Montsant, Catalonia

(PATRICIA R. SOTO/ICEX)

Restaurants either side of La Rambla offer a cornucopia of variety.

For special food and wine outside La Boqueria, try Freixa Tradició and Can Ravell. Make sure you walk through the shop of the latter to a spiral staircase that takes you to the splendid upstairs that has catered to Barcelona's cognoscenti since 1929. Do walk around **La Barceloneta** district for casual tapas and Gracia for wine bars.

When wandering around the city, make sure you go in search of the works of local architect **Antoni Gaudí** (1852–1926). His La Pedrera and Casa Batlló are works of art in a category called *Modernisme*, which is like a mix between Art Nouveau and Art Deco. His **Sagrada Familia** church divides opinions but is unmistakably Catalan.

People-watching along La Rambla is more entertaining than many things you have to pay for, and catching a glimpse of locals dancing *sardana* on Sunday morning in front of the Gothic cathedral in the medieval heart of the city is unforgettable. With its magnificent airport, port and marina facilities, Barcelona is the perfect starting point for a wine tour of the region.

FOR FURTHER INFORMATION

A good place to start is www.barcelona-on-line.es

Wine shops

Lavinia
Avda Diagonal, 605
08028 Barcelona
Tel: 933 634 445
www.lavinia.com

Vila Viniteca
Calle Agullers, 7
08003 Barcelona.
Tel: 902 327 777
www.vilaviniteca.es

History

Catalonia's history as a wine producer dates back at least to the era of Phoenician and Greek traders. It was during Roman suzerainty that the industry began to prosper, exporting wines with such success that new vineyard plantings were banned by Rome to protect its own domestic producers. These foundations suffered from centuries of disuse during the Visigothic and Moorish occupations. The 11th century

witnessed the beginning of a long, slow recovery following the establishment of the Kingdom of Aragón and then unification with Castile in 1469.

Golden Age

Catalan wine began a golden age from the final quarter of the 19th century. Income from selling wine to phylloxera-hit France combined with earnings from satellite industries such as cork production and glass manufacturing led to great prosperity. Vineyards were planted in virtually every adequate plot of land. When the Pyrenees failed to halt the onslaught of phylloxera as had been expected and hoped, wine production

(HEINZ HEBEISEN/ICEX)

Once a fishing village set amid rocky coves, Cadaqués has in more recent times inspired artists and writers such as Salvador Dalí and Federico García Lorca

was cut by more than half and numerous grape farmers were left destitute.

The Cava boom

Cava (Spanish sparkling wine) was first made in 1872 by Codorníu, a company headed by Josep Raventós. Five years later Codorníu succeeded in replacing Veuve Clicquot Champagne at Spanish royal banquets. Although phylloxera devastated production, Cava was established as a Spanish product.

Many Catalans would enjoy a bottle of *semi-seco* (dryish) or *dulce* (sweet) Cava accompanied by sweet pastries on the way home from Mass on Sundays.

Eventually, with the emergence of competition—exemplified by Freixenet—Cava was to burst onto world markets and become an international success. This boom transformed winemaking in the northeast.

Cava's regulations are peculiar in that it can be legally produced in a number of different geographic locations, including Penedès, Rioja, Navarra, Ribera del Duero, Aragón and Utiel-Requena. However, almost all Cava is produced in Catalonia, with 75 percent sourced from around the district of Sant Sadurní d'Anoia, 50 km (30 miles) west of Barcelona on the AP-2, then the AP-7 (take exit 27).

Bottles carry the word *Cava* on the label. Corks have a four-pointed star on the flat base. Cava must undergo a second fermentation within the bottle in which it will later be sold, as in the case of Champagne, and must be aged for a minimum of nine months before being sold. The words *Cava Gran Reserva* on the label indicate that the wine has spent a minimum of 30 months aging in bottle before being sold. A Consejo Regulador regulates production.

Removido *or riddling*

During the nine months of aging, the wine undergoes *removido*, a process that begins with bottles in a horizontal position and slowly turns and riddles them until they are upside down with their internal sediment lying on the cork. This is done by hand or in large racks known as *girasoles* (literally, sunflowers). Bottles are then disgorged in a dramatic process called *degüelle* where they are uncorked and the yeasty sediment removed. They are then topped up with *licor de expedición*, a mixture of still wine and sugar syrup, and re-corked.

Cava Styles

The amount of sugar syrup added determines the level of sweetness, hence the style of the wine. Brut Nature has virtually no

sugar added and is bone
dry. Extra Brut has less
than 6 grams of sugar
added per liter. Brut has
6–15 grams per liter. Extra
Seco (extra dry) has 12–20
grams. Seco (dry) has 17–35
grams added. Semi-Seco
(semi-dry) has 33–50 grams
per liter. The richly sweet
Dulce (sweet), which is
usually served with dessert,
has over 50 grams per liter.

Other Catalan wine regions

Excluding Cava, Catalu
nya (as Catalonia is called
in Catalan) has 11 DOs:
Alella; Ampurdán-Costa
Brava; Cataluña; Conca de
Barberà; Costers del Segre;
Montsant; Penedès; Pla del
Bages; Priorat; Tarragona;
Terra Alta. Together they
cover around 83,000 hec-
tares (more than 200,000
acres).

Ampurdán and Alella

Ampurdán-Costa Brava is
the most northerly denomination in Spain, immedi-
ately south of the French
border and planted primarily with Garnacha (including Blanca) and Cariñena

grapes. The main reason to
visit this area is the beauty
of its setting. This is one of
the oldest wine-producing
regions in the country, with
the first vines planted at
least by the 5th century BC.
Winemaking blossomed
under Greek influence
around the colony of Roses
and during Roman times in
Empúries. Later consolida-
tion occurred under ecclesi-
astical orders in the Middle
Ages. Catalan wine reached
a peak of prosperity when
its wines were served at the
French court. Phylloxera
dealt it a blow from which a
lot of regions outside those
involved in today's Cava
production have struggled to
recover.

There is plenty of
evidence of this former
glory. Take the steep and
winding road from Roses
to Cadaqués on the Cap de
Creus promontory and you
can see the remains of carefully constructed terraces
on which vines were once
planted and painstakingly
tended. Some vineyards
reached down to the water's
edge and some, so locals will
tell you, were so inaccessible
that they had to be har-
vested from the sea and the
grapes transported by boat.

Towns like Capmany,

(HAROLD HECKLE)

Alvaro Palacios, whose Priorat wines are among the most expensive and highly-prized in Spain

Mollet, Espolla, Ricardell and Pont de Molins have cooperatives advertising their wines. The region is a great spot for a holiday and visitors are welcomed. Although situated on the crowded Costa Brava, it is well to the north of the mass tourist areas. With a base on the coast, several pleasant excursions can be made. Cadaqués, a small town on the coast, is well worth a visit. So too are the archeological site of Empúries and the lovely if eccentric old town of Figueres. The wine country is a mere 30-minute drive from the coast and a pleasant day can be spent visiting the cooperatives and the town of Perelada, home of the leading Cavas Castillo de Perelada.

Perelada

The town of Perelada is dominated by a 14th-century complex of buildings including the **Carmen de Perelada** church with its charming Gothic cloister and the Castle-Palace with its two crenellated towers. Underground cellars have aged wine here since the church's foundation and now house a worthwhile wine museum. The owners of the castle, the family that once built luxury Hispano-Suiza cars, produce wine in many parts of Catalonia. They have a five-star wine spa hotel and golf course that, while not cheap, is certainly spectacular. You can enjoy great wines and food in a fabulous setting here.

Cadaqués

This seaside village has been a magnet to aristocrats, bohemians and painters (Salvador Dalí lived in Port Lligat, in the northern bay) since the beginning of the 20th century. Its **Marítim** and **Casa Anita** bars

are worth visiting. Both are in the center and the latter displays drawings by Dalí and Pablo Picasso.

Figueres

This small city about 100 km (60 miles) north of Barcelona is famous for being the birthplace of Salvador Dalí. Here the artist created his biggest surrealist work: the **Teatre Museu Gala Salvador Dalí.**

ATTRACTIONS

Gala-Salvador Dalí Foundation
Torre Galatea
Pujada del Castell, 28
17600 Figueres
Tel: 972 677 505

House-Museum Salvador Dalí
Portlligat
17489 Cadaqués
Tel: 972 251 015
www.salvador-dali.org

Sant Pau

On the C-32 coast road between Barcelona and Ampurdán is the Restaurant Sant Pau, one of the country's best eateries, owned and run by

Carme Ruscalleda, the first woman chef in Spain to win gastronomy's top accolade, three Michelin stars. Do book first for an unforgettable seaside food and wine experience. Note that Ruscalleda runs an exact copy, serving the same menu daily, in Tokyo—a unique feat at this almost unimaginable level of gastronomic perfection.

Santi Santamaría

Another three-Michelin-star chef, Santi Santamaría, is a strong critic of "molecular" or technique-oriented cuisine. His ingredients-led style had gained him worldwide recognition as one of the best cooks active today. His restaurant, **Can Fabes**, just north of the AP-7 between Ampurdán and Barcelona is another absolute must.

Alella

This denomination, just over half an hour's drive north of Barcelona, is of note mainly because it has managed to survive despite being encroached upon by Barcelona's urban and industrial sprawl. These days you can almost say it

is a wine region within a city. With just 550 hectares (1,350 acres), it is one of the smallest wine denominations in the world.

Two bodegas are worth visiting. **Alella Vinícola**, the region's cooperative hails from 1886 when the region would have presented quite a different sight. The façade celebrated its centenary in 2006, yet behind it is a modern winery dating from the 1990s. **Marqués de Alella** (owned by the Parxet group) is a typically modern Catalan enterprise, producing interesting wines and Cavas.

BODEGAS & MORE

DO Alella
Masia Museu
Can Magarola
Av Sant Mateu 2
08328 Alella
Tel: 93 555 91 53
(It's not easy to raise a response, I've found.)

ALELLA
Alella Vinícola
Calle Àngel Guimerà, 62
08328 Alella
Tel: 93 540 3842
comercial@alellavinicola.com
www.alellavinicola.com

(IGNACIO MUÑOZ-SECA/ICEX)

Inside the old labeling room at the art nouveau building of Bodegas Codorníu in San Sadurní d'Anoia

PERELADA

Castillo Perelada
Vinos y Cavas
Plaça del Carme, 1
17491 Perelada
Tel: 93 223 3022
perelada@castilloperelada.com
www.grupperalada.com

TIANA

Marqués de Alella
Mas Parxet
08391 Tiana
Tel: 93 395 08 11
info@marquesdealella.com
www.marquesdealella.com

Penedès and Cava

The history of Penedès is not unlike that of Spain's other Mediterranean wine regions. What sets it apart is its strong recovery from phylloxera in the 20th century. Today it is one of Spain's most prosperous white wine producers as well as being the home of Cava, one of the outstanding success stories of the Spanish wine industry.

Cava's rise

When Josep Raventós perfected Spain's celebrated sparkling wine in 1872, red wine was the region's main product. Such was the success of Cava that when the vineyards were replanted after phylloxera, it was mostly with white varieties. Large factory-size wineries producing base wine exclusively for Cava began to dot remote spots in the

(HAROLD HECKLE)

Hand harvesting at Bodegas Torres' Priorat vineyard set on Licorella crushed slate soils in Porrera

countryside. These vast establishments fed, and feed, Cava producers with the raw material with which to make fizzy wine. Red wines have made an impressive comeback but base wine for Cava followed by white still wine claim a major part of the market.

Cava's success has elevated it to become the second best selling sparkling wine in the world after Champagne. Cava is recognized in every corner of the globe. Its appetite for grapes and base wine is almost insatiable and many small grape-growers, winemakers and cooperatives make a substantial living supplying it. The huge earnings generated have

percolated down through the entire agricultural and commercial structure of Catalonia and have led to enormous investment both in the region and across the world.

Grape varieties

The Penedès Valley has a consistent climate at three altitude levels: sea level; valley floor; and slopes (Alto Penedès). The predominant white grapes Parellada, Macabeo (Viura) and Xarel-lo make relatively good blends for sparkling wine. There has been a big debate as to whether introducing French (or international) varieties such as Chardonnay and Pinot Noir is a valid option or whether it reduces the "native" character of autochthonous (indigenous) blends.

Vilafranca del Penedès

While Sant Sadurní is the Cava capital, Vilafranca del Penedès, about 40 km (25 miles) from central Barcelona on the Tarragona road and with an exit on the AP-7, is the regional center of still wine production. It is a prosperous rural town with a wine museum, some reasonable hotels (although travellers may prefer to stay at the vibrant beach resort of Sitges), good shops and some excellent restaurants. Villagers are famous throughout Catalonia for their *casteller* skills that involve building astonishing human towers seven persons tall.

Wine museum and Consejo Regulador

The wine museum is housed in the palace of the Kings of Aragón, dating back to the 12th century. As well as having an unrivalled display of viti- and vinicultural equipment, it has sections on art, archeology

and ceramics. It also has a bar stocked with most of the wines made in the region. The Consejo Regulador is a modern building to the south west of town, near the highway.

FOR FURTHER INFORMATION
The Town Hall has its own very useful website: www.ajvilafranca.es

Tourism center Oficina Municipal de Turisme, Cort 14, 08720 Vilafranca del Penedès
Tel: 938 181 254
turisme@ajvilafranca.es
www.turismevilafranca.com

Consell Regulador of the Penedes Origin Denomination Plaça Àgora, 1 08720 Vilafranca del Penedès. Tel: 938 904 811
dopenedes@dopenedes.es
www.dopenedes.es

Bodegas Torres

The leading still wine producer of the region is the internationally famous Bodegas Torres, whose old winery on Calle del Comercio near the railway station can still be visited by appointment. Under the direction of Miguel

(HAROLD HECKLE)

The author holds a basket of edible mushrooms freshly picked in the foothills of the Pyrenees, Catalonia

Agustín Torres, a brilliant winemaker of world renown, this company has become one of Spain's flagship wine companies and a member of Primum Familiae Vini, an international association of some of the world's greatest wine producers. Incredibly, Torres was responsible for kick-starting modern winemaking in Chile and is also behind a successful Californian project (run by his sister Marimar Torres) in the Russian River region.

A few years ago Torres bought another pioneering Spanish winery, Jean Leon, which had been founded in Penedès by a prominent Californian restaurateur of Spanish ancestry. Jean Leon had been a close friend of actor James Dean and catered to Ronald Reagan's White House. Torres has an impressive visitors' center and a sort of secret restaurant set among vines that is sometimes open to dedicated wine lovers. You have to make serious overtures for access to the restaurant, though.

Make sure you get to try **Grans Muralles**, one of the most extraordinary Spanish wine projects of recent years. Miguel Agustín recovered some rare grapes and planted them behind the medieval walls of the Cistercian monastery of Poblet, where some of the kings of Catalonia are buried. This is over the mountains in neighboring DO Conca de Barberà and the wine is made from Monastrell, Garnacha Tinta, very old Cariñena and recovered historic varieties Garró and Samsó. Also ask to try the blockbuster **Milmanda** made from Chardonnay. Interestingly, Torres makes no Cava.

Other still wine producers

Most noteworthy bodegas are outside the town and almost all specialize in white wines, with Cava as a constant presence in the cellars. One of the most charming is **Huguet de Can Feixes**, located in a beautiful old fortified farmhouse. Once there you can easily imagine farmers through the centuries fighting off Moors and other raiders. They make some deep and supple red wine from Merlot and Cabernet Sauvignon as well as Cava and *blanco* (white).

One of the most colorful characters making wine in Penedès is Carlos Esteva, who moved into his grandfather's estate at **Can Ràfols dels Caus** and hasn't looked back since. He makes white wines and Cavas, of course, but some of his reds, made from Pinot Noir, Merlot and Syrah, are notable, and the old farmhouse is a delight.

Among the most impressive wineries in the region is **Raventós i Blanc**, built by one of the senior heirs to the Codorníu fortune who split from the rest of the family and made his winery more or less on the doorstep of the historic Cava bodega. While this step may have been to thumb his nose at the rest of the family, the Cavas made here are very good, as you would expect. Some of the still wines are also worthy of note. Remember, red wine, or *tinto*, is called *Negre* in Catalan.

One of the most dedicated viticultural researchers in the area is **Josep Maria Albet i Noya**, who set up his winery with his brother Antoni and the help of their mother, Núria Noya i Rafecas. There is a charge for their guided vineyard and winery tours, but it is a small price to pay if you want a truly in-depth and personalized experience of winemaking and grapegrowing in the region.

Sant Martí Sarroca

Sant Martí, west-northwest of Vilafranca on the BP-2121, has a lovely Romanesque church and, from the square in front, there is an incomparable view across the rolling terrain of Penedès with its vineyards and wineries right to the jagged peaked outline of Montserrat.

Cava country

The C-243 road from Vilafranca del Penedès to Sant Sadurní d'Anoia is just 12.7 kilometers (7.9 miles), a 17-minute drive; except during harvest time. Then, long processions of tractors hauling grapes to the crushers will turn a simple drive into an endlessly fascinating odyssey that can see you sitting in traffic for long stretches of the day.

Sant Sadurní d'Anoia

While Sant Sadurní d'Anoia might not be the most exciting or beautiful town, a visit is a must. On its outskirts is the giant **Codorníu** winery, among the most architecturally imposing bodegas in Spain. Built by José María

(HEINZ HEBEISEN/ICEX)

The ancient wine cellars of the Cistercian monastery at Poblet, Tarragona, founded in 1151. Many kings of Catalonia were buried at this monastery, which is open to the public

Puig i Cadafalch at the end of the 19th century, it is a leading example of *modernisme* and is a national monument. It rises amid beautifully laid-out gardens and beneath it are five underground levels of cellars extending for a total of 26 km (16 miles) through which visitors are transported in miniature trains. The

winery also has an impressive wine museum.

Codorníu also owns the **Masía Bach** winery, which produces value-for-money still wine. Housed in an old *masía*, or country house, it is located in Sant Esteve Sesrovires close to Sant Sadurní. Ask for directions at Codorníu.

Freixenet (pronounced 'Frey-shen-et') is Codorníu's arch rival. It is also the largest single sparkling wine producer in the world. Its massive bodega also welcomes visitors and is located near the railway station in Sant Sadurní. While more workmanlike, you cannot fail to be impressed by the sheer scale of the operation.

You will need lunch after visiting these two giants and the **Mirador de les Caves** just outside Sant Sadurní provides the perfect location with its wonderful hillside views over the vineyards across to Montserrat.

Rovellats in La Bleda, near Sant Martí Sarroca, is a smaller winery with a wonderful 15th-century *masía*. The larger **Segura Viudas**, now owned by Freixenet, has an even older *masía* dating back to the 11th century.

BODEGAS & MORE

VILAFRANCA DEL PENEDÈS

Torres
Miguel Torres i Carbó 6
08720 Vilafranca del
Penedès
Tel: 938 177 400
(Vinyet Almirall)
valmirall@torres.es
www.torres.es

SUBIRATS

Albet i Noya
Can Vendrell de la Codina
Sant Pau D'Ordal
08739 Subirats
Tel: 938 994 812
albetinoya@albetinoya.com
www.albetinoya.com

CAN RÀFOLS DELS CAUS

Can Ràfols dels Caus
Avinyonet del Penedès
Tel: 938 970 013
canrafolsdelscaus@canra-
folsdelscaus.com
www.canrafolsdelscaus.com

SANT SADURNÍ D'ANOIA

Codorníu
Ctra Capellades Km 20
08635 Sant Esteve
Sesrovires
Tel: 937 714 052
codinfo@codorniu.com
www.codorniu.es

Gramona
Av de les Casetes de
Can Mir s/n
08770 Sant Sadurní
D'Anoia
Tel: 938 910 113
cava@gramona.com
www.gramona.com

**Josep María
Raventós i Blanc**
Afores s/n
08770 Sant Sadurní
D'Anoia
Tel: 938 183 262
raventos@raventos.com
www.raventos.com

Juvé & Camps
Ctra Gelida s/n
08770 Sant Sadurní d'Anoia
Tel: 938 911 000
juveycamps@juveycamps.com
www.troc.es/juveycamps

CABRERA D'ANOIA

Huguet de Can Feixes
Can Feixas
08785 Canaletes
Tel: 937 718 227
canfeixes@canfeixes.com
www.canfeixes.com

SANT MARTÍ SARROCA

Rovellats
08731 La Bleda
Tel: 934 880 575
rovellats@cavasrovellats.com
www.cavasrovellats.com

(GNACIO MUÑOZ-SECA/ICEX)

View of Sant Sadurní d'Anoia, the capital of Cava country, with the Montserrat Mountains in the background

TORRELAVIT

Segura Viudas
Heredad Segura Viudas
Tel: 938 997 227
gabriel.suberviola@freixenet.es
www.freixenet.es

The Raimat Estate

Heading out of Vilafranca del Penedès on the AP-2 (until exit 9) you will reach DO Costers del Segre, which was granted its status in 1988. Note that the Poblet monastery is directly south on the small T-232 road. This region was almost certainly granted its DO to give a boost to the

Raventós family's investment in the Raimat estate. When Manuel Raventós, owner of Codorníu, bought Raimat towards the beginning of the last century it was described as "3,000 hectares (7,500 acres) with a castle and one tree." Like much of the surrounding landscape it resembled a desert, due to lack of rainfall. Years of work transformed it into what the Spanish government has called "a model agricultural estate."

Raventós constructed a canal to bring water and removed nearby hills. When the soil proved to have too high a salt content he planted fruit trees to help leach it out. Today the estate has 1,500 hectares (3,700 acres) of vineyards and a similar area planted with fruit trees and cereals. As befits a project of Edwardian scope, the property has its own railway station and workers' village with a football field. The old winery, dating from 1918, has been complemented by another completed in 1988 and built in the shape of a pyramid with grass growing on its slopes.

Raimat produces some interesting wines and Cavas. Its vineyards are planted with a wide selection of local and imported grape varieties and its winemakers use all the latest winemaking technology. A visit should be combined with a tour of the medieval

A vineyard worker trains vines in the DO Montsant, Catalonia

(PATRICIA R. SOTO/ICEX)

monastery of Poblet and Torres' Grans Muralles vineyard.

RAIMAT

Make an appointment at **Grupo Codorníu** Apartado de correos 200 08950 Esplugues de Llobregat, Barcelona Tel: 935 051 551 info@raimat.es www.raimat.com or **Bodegas Raimat** Carretera Lleida s/n 25111 Raimat, Lleida Tel: 973 724 000

Priorat and the mountains of Catalonia

Tarragona

Tarragona is a quiet provincial city with good hotels and restaurants, a fine *rambla* (parade) that leads to a *mirador* or viewpoint over the sea and a lovely medieval quarter. This is a perfect place from which to witness the grandeur of Spain's glorious Roman past. Don't forget that Spain was the birthplace of two of Rome's greatest emperors: Trajan and Hadrian.

In the 18th century great wine trading businesses established offices near the port here and bought wine from producers and cooperatives in the interior, improving and exporting it. Today most of these firms have disappeared. This is a good place from which to explore the mountainous wine regions nearby.

The interior

The roads leading to and around Priorat can be steep and windy so if you tend to suffer from carsickness, be warned. However, the beauty of the scenery will more than compensate for any discomfort. From Tarragona take the N420 to Reus and continue in the direction of Falset. The road begins to climb after Reus, providing some spectacular views, before reaching a pass and then descending to the wine town of Falset. From here you can choose to go north to Porrera, then northwest to Torroja del Priorat then, following a roughly circular route, Gratallops, or vice

A view over the steeply banked vineyards on Licorella crushed slate soils at Poblet, Priorat, during harvest time

versa. Gratallops is the heart of modern wine-making Priorat.

Priorat

Priorat takes is name from a priory, Priorato de Scala Dei (Priory of the Stairway of God) dating from the arrival of an Order of Carthusian monks in 12th century.

Codorníu now owns a winery in the tiny settlement of Scala Dei. The sheer beauty of the wild, rugged surrounding landscape of jagged peaks and crushed slate stone outcrops with their dark, vaguely metallic sheen is captivating. The little villages built hugging steep mountain slopes—many of which were being aban-

(HAROLD HECKLE)

doned until wine brought some measure of prosperity back to the region—and the abandoned lead mines all date back to Roman times.

The rediscovery of the winemaking potential of the region, thanks to its slate soils, was made by Catalan winemaker René Barbier. Barbier talked a group of fellow wine lovers, including Carles Pastrana of Clos de l' Obac;

Álvaro Palacios, famed for L'Ermita; José Lluis Perez of Clos Martinet and father of winemaker Sarah Perez; and Daphne Glorian, owner of Clos Erasmus. These were the founders of this now world-renowned wine region. All of these vineyards have become places of vinicultural pilgrimage in recent years.

The region had been dying fast. Its climate and

soil produce some of the best olive oil, figs and hazelnuts in Spain, and some of its most distinctive wines. But the low yield of its fruit trees and vines, often planted on almost inaccessible and hard-to-tend slopes and steep valley terraces, made it difficult to earn a living from the land. Young people tradition-ally departed to the bright lights of cities or coastal resorts, leaving the region to the old, a few eccentrics and the occasional tourist.

The success of projects like Palacios' L'Ermita changed all that. Money has begun flowing back and Priorat wines now feature in the best wine lists of the finest restaurants and hotels around the world. Palacios and his friends bought some of the oldest vines on terraces that had seen monks tending them. Modern wineries have found it hard to copy the painstakingly handmade stone terraces of old and some have opted for much less picturesque terraces carved by bulldozers. To-day the old Garnacha and Samsó (Mazuelo) vines that are wonderfully impervious to the sparse mineral quali-ties of the slate have been

bolstered with some new varieties, namely Syrah. The DO has 11 sub-regions that in 2008 produced 4,795,721 kg (10.5 million lbs) of grapes, according to official figures.

Wine lovers with a penchant for music should check out **Celler Vall-Llach** in Porrera. It belongs to Catalan singer-songwriter Lluis Llach who defied the Fascist dictatorship of General Francisco Franco (1939-75) by singing politically-charged songs in Catalan when the language (and all cultural manifesta-tions of a Catalan identity) were banned or opposed by the regime. Aware of the potential in the region, Torres has inaugurated the first winery it has designed outside Penedès in Priorat. Don't miss it, with its mag-nificent views across the deep valley landscape.

Montsant

Literally surrounding Priorat is DO Montsant, previously known as Falset. To many, especially the supermarket chains, this region is like a cut-price Priorat. It is worth sniffing out for that reason.

(HAROLD HECHLE)

Freshly picked Cep mushrooms on sale at La Boquería market in central Barcelona

FOR FURTHER INFORMATION

Priorat Tourism Office
Sant Marcel, 2
43730 Falset
Tel: 977 831 023
www.turismepriorat.org

DO Priorat
Carrer Major 2
43737 Torroja del Priorat
Tel: 977 839 495
info@doqpriorat.org
www.doqpriorat.org

DO Montsant
For travel and visit advice please refer to: http://prioratwines.com/montsant

Tarragona tourist guide:
www.tarragonaguide.com
to the port:
www.porttarragona.es
One useful date to keep in mind is that Priorat celebrates its annual Wine Fair the first weekend of May.

BODEGAS & MORE

Alvaro Palacios
Polígon 6, Parcela 26
43737 Gratallops
Tel: 977 839 195
info@alvaropalacios.com

Clos de l'Obac
Camí Manyetes s/n
43737 Gratallops
Tel: 977 839 276
info@costersdelsiurana.com
www.costersdelsiurana.com

Clos Mogador
Camí Manyetes s/n
43737 Gratallops
Tel: 97 783 9171
closmogador@closmogador.com
www.closmogador.com

PORRERA

Celler Vall-Llach
Calle Pont 9
43739 Porrera
Tel: 977 828 244
celler@vallllach.com
www.vallllach.com

Cims de Porrera
Crta de Torroja s/n
43739 Porrera
Tel: 977 828 233
info@cimsdeporrera.com

SCALA DEI

Cellers de Scala Dei Rbla
Cartoixa s/n, Scala Dei
Tel: 977 827 027

cellers@teleline.es
www.grupocodorniu.com

EL MOLAR

De Muller, SA
Mas de les Puces
43736 El Molar
Tel: 977 756 265
nacional@demuller.es
www.demuller.es

EL LLOAR

Torres Priorat
Finca la Solteta s/n
43737 El Lloar
valmirall@torres.es
www.torres.es

Clos Martinet
Mas Martinet.
Ctra de Falset a Gratallops
Km 6, Falset
masmartinet@masmartinet.com
www.masmartinet.com

Catalan Cuisine

Next to the Basque region, Catalonia is considered to have the most varied and sophisticated cuisine in Spain. Many top chefs source their ingredients seasonally and adapt their menus accordingly.

Fresh ingredients

The coast produces good fish, which is traditionally

served in a stew such as the *Sarsuela* or grilled with sauces in the excellent *Parrilladas*. Fresh fish cooked to your taste on a sizzling hot piece of slate (*a la llosa*) is a fabulous way to accompany a good white wine. Further inland the more wooded areas yield an abundance of small game, herbs, mushrooms (particularly the unique *rovellons*) and the very popular pine nuts. Veal, chicken, goose and pork are all used, the last being the basis of the typical *botifarra* sausages, with pine nuts, cinnamon, almonds and cumin.

Catalan sauces

Sauces are a great Catalan specialty. They include the famous *allioli*, made with garlic and olive oil; *romesco* sauce of Tarragona, which can be very spicy, and is made with garlic, small peppers, tomatoes, bread and roasted almonds; *sanfaina*, with sautéed onions, eggplant, zucchini and tomatoes; and *picada*, with saffron, garlic, hazelnuts, almonds, parsley and cinnamon. These are served either to accompany grilled shellfish, fish or meat, or form the basis of a Catalan stew such as the famous *Romesco de Peix*.

Specialties

Arròs Negre which literally means "black rice" is one of Catalonia's answers to paella. It is rice cooked in a large, two-handled frying pan with shellfish and it derives its color from squid, whose dark ink gives the dish its fabulous sheen.

Fideuà is one Catalonia's most popular dishes. Thin fried noodles are boiled in flavorful fish broth with many of the ingredients typical of paella. Traditionally it is served with a helping of tangy *allioli*.

Faves a la Catalana are broad beans stewed in white wine with black *butifarra*, and thick slices of bacon and onions.

Anec amb Figues is a typical dish of Ampurdán made with duck roasted in a little brandy, or sherry, with figs.

Sarsuela de mariscos is one of the classic dishes of Catalonia. It is a fish casserole that can be extremely elaborate. Some chefs use only shellfish such as clams, mussels, shrimp and lobster. Others mix in chunks of fish such as hake.

WHERE TO STAY AND EAT

Barcelona

Can Ravell
Carrer Aragó, 313
08009 Barcelona
Tel: 93 457 51 14 or
        93 457 51 16
www.ravell.com (R)

Freixa Tradició
Sant Elies 22
08006 Barcelona
Tel: 93 209 75 59
info@freixatradicio.com
www.freixatradicio.com (R)

**Perelada Castillo Perelada
Vinos y Cavas**
Plaça del Carme 1
17491 Peralada
Tel: 93 223 3022
perelada@castilloperelada.com
www.grupperalada.com (H/R)

Sant Celoni Can Fabes
Sant Joan 6
08470 Sant Celoni
Tel: 34 938 672 851
canfabes@canfabes.com
www.canfabes.com (R)

Sant Pau

Restaurant Sant Pau
Carrer nou, 10
08395 Sant Pol de Mar
Tel: 93 760 06 62
santpau@ruscalleda.cat
www.ruscalleda.com

Tarragona

AC Tarragona
Avda de Roma, 8
43005 Tarragona
Tel: 977 247 105
actarragona@ac-hotels.com
www.ac-hotels.com (H/R)

Husa Imperial Tarraco
Passeig Palmeres s/n
43003 Tarragona
Tel: 977 233 040
hotelimperialtarraco@husa.es
www.hotelhusaimperialtarraco.com
(H/R)

Hotel Ciutat de Tarragona
Plaza Imperial Tarraco, 5
43005 Tarragona
Tel: 977 250 999
www.hotelciutatdetarragona.com
(H/R)

**Vilafranca del Penedès
Hotel Alfa Penedès (****)**
Calle Font de les Graus
nº 2, 08720 Vilafranca
del Penedès
Tel: 938 172 026
www.alfahotel.com

**Hotel Casa Torner i Guell
(*****)** Rambla de Sant
Francesco, 26
08720 Vilafranca del
Penedès
Tel: 938 174 755
www.casatorneriguell.com

Hotel Domo (****)
Francesc Macià 4
08720 Vilafranca del
Penedès

Tel. 938 172 4 26
info@domohotel.com
www.domohotel.com

(FERNANDO BRIONES/ICEX)

**Cava producer Bodega Segura cultivates Macabeo, Parellada and Xarel.
lo varieties in Sant Sadurní d´Anoia**

Bodegas Hermanos Pérez
Pascua, makers of Viña
Pedrosa, Ribera del Duero

CASTILE

ASTILLA, THE BEATING HEART OF SPAIN as a former world superpower, takes its name from the many castles that dot its countryside and emblazon its heraldic symbols. It was from Castile that Christian rulers pushed south to re-conquer Islamic Al-Andalus and forge a united Spain. The marriage of Isabel (Isabella), Queen of Castile, to King Ferdinand of Aragón in 1469 paved the way for the defeat of Granada—the last Moorish bastion in the Iberian Peninsula. Today, this ancient land in the northern half of the country is called Castilla-León. Further south you will find the larger Castilla-La Mancha, made up of lands south of Madrid captured by Castile in 1085.

Castilla-León is rich in the legacy of what became one of history's great empires. Medieval walled cities, countless palaces, libraries, churches and monasteries all give testament to the once unstoppable power of Spain. And for equally intriguing reasons, the wines here are regarded as among the best in the country.

Castilla-León (sometimes referred to as *Castilla la vieja* or Old Castile) sits on a *meseta*, the highest plateau in Europe. Much of this is over 600 meters (2000 ft) above sea level and the climate can be extreme. Temperatures rise to over 40°C (104°F) in summer and plunge to -20°C (-4°F) in winter. It is often said that Castile only has two seasons—*invierno e infierno* (winter and hell)—because both spring and autumn can be very short, in unlucky years just a matter of days. (Hay fever sufferers be warned. Because spring is so short all sorts of pollen explode into the air at this time. Come prepared.)

Valladolid—the perfect hub

At the height of its imperial grandeur, when Spain ruled much of Europe, the Americas and the Philippines, the capital was located in Valladolid. With the royal court

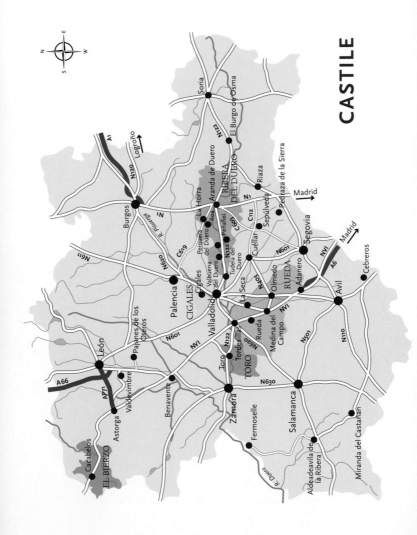

CASTILE

(MIGUEL S. MOÑITA/ICEX)

Legendary winemaker Mariano García with his sons Alberto and Eduardo. Mariano García made Vega Sicilia for 30 years before branching out to Aalto, Mauro and Maurodos

as clients, regional wine producers made special efforts to discover (in many cases re-discover) the best locations for growing quality grapes. It comes as no surprise that today Valladolid is located within easy reach of Castilla-León's best wine regions. It makes a perfect base from which to plan excursions. For those who want to begin their journey from Valladolid, it is now possible to fly direct into Villanubla international airport, or to catch a bullet train called TGV (*tren de gran velocidad*) from Madrid straight to its central station. The city has all the attractions you would expect of a former imperial capital:

an imposing main square; fabulous monuments; and excellent restaurants, some of them housed in beautiful and historic buildings.

You can also drive from Rioja following the AP-1 through Burgos, another of Spain's former capitals. From Burgos the E-80 takes you straight to Valladolid. **AC Palacio De Santa Ana** is a fine hotel built in the shell of a monastery dating from the 18th century and is a 10-minute drive from the city center next to the Espanidad bridge. It has ample parking and a great restaurant as well as a pool and fitness center. The **Hotel Imperial** is located in a 16th-century historic building, perfectly restored and full of charm, next to the Plaza Major. Try the **Restaurante mil vinos.** The name says it all—1000 wines—and its wine list really is amazing. It's a good place to begin the evening. Try a few wines, eat some tapas and then move on to a sit-down meal.

For those who don't mind driving a little further and who prefer countryside quiet to the bustle and excitement of a city, **Parador de Tordesillas** is a good bet. Tordesillas is a historic little town built on a hill 35 km (22 miles) southwest of Valladolid on the E-80. It was here that Spain and Portugal negotiated a division of America (the New World) between them in 1494. The **Convent of Santa Clara**, where Joanna the Mad

(d. 1555) was imprisoned by her son Charles V, is worth a visit.

FOR FURTHER INFORMATION

Airport
Carretera N-601 Km 203
47620 Villanubla
Valladolid
Airport code: VLL
Tel: 983 415 500

The Wines of Castile

The wine industry of Castile dates back at least to the 4th century BC. Ancient wine-related artifacts have been found at a settlement called Pintia at Padilla de Duero just west of Peñafiel and immediately north of the N-122. The town of Medina del

Bodegas Aalto, Ribera del Duero

(HAROLD HECKLE)

Campo boasted some 470 wine merchants in the 13th century and by the late 15th century such was the fame of local *tinto* that Columbus is said to have taken casks of Toro wine aboard the *Pinta* on his first great voyage of discovery.

Subsequently the industry was laid low by three body blows. First, king Philip II moved the court to Madrid. Then, at the turn of the 19th century, came phylloxera, devastating the vineyards. Finally, at the end of the Civil War in the late 1930s, new Wheat Laws were passed to encourage wheat production.

One towering beacon of quality survived: Bodegas Vega Sicilia, for decades considered one of Spain's best wines. The entire region has in recent years turned around to produce some magnificent wines following in the wake of this winery just to the east of Valladolid.

Ribera del Duero

The region's largest DO has grown around the reputation of Vega Sicilia and some extraordinary wines that have emerged. Vega Sicilia Unico is a large and imposing wine. Luxuriously perfumed and with a wonderful balance between concentrated, fragrant fruit and an oakiness acquired after painstaking barrel aging, these wines have always enjoyed immense prestige around the world.

The principal grape of the region is Tinto Fino, a Tempranillo clone. A fair number of wineries, including Vega Sicilia, blend in small quantities of Merlot, Cabernet Sauvignon and Malbec.

Cigales

Just to the north of Valladolid is a surprising find: Cigales, overlooking the city in the distance. Mariano García, for 30 years winemaker at Vega Sicilia, has called the *terroir* here some of the best in Spain. Modern winemakers produce some delightful wines, full of character and finesse.

Toro

To the west, across the border in the province of Zamora, lies Toro, another region that has shot to fame in recent years due to the outstanding quality of its wines. Once, these wines

Rueda only authorizes white wine production; these are Verdejo grapes for Bodegas Oro de Castilla

were considered a bit rustic, thick with heavy tannins. Today, Toro's wines are among Spain's best.

Rueda

Rueda has become famous for aromatic, refreshing white wines. The arrival in 1972 of Rioja's famous Marqués de Riscal winery heralded a revolution in quality white production.

Ribera del Duero was granted DO status in 1982 and now boasts more than 200 bodegas, including some of Spain's most for-ward-looking and exciting wineries. The name means Banks of the Duero river, and the region stretches from El Burgo de Osma to Tudela de Duero.

The valley contains a wealth of soil and subsoil deposits which, when combined with its special micro-climates, gives wines of exceptional quality. Ribera del Duero does not list white wine, just luscious reds and some *rosados*.

Before you set off, it's a good idea to examine the DO's website carefully. It contains an up-to-date list

(PH LIP CLARK)

of all wineries and has all the contact details you will need.

FOR FURTHER INFORMATION
Consejo Regulador de la DO Ribera del Duero
Calle Hospital, 6
09300 Roa (Burgos)
Tel: 947 541 221
www.riberadelduero.es

As you drive out of Valladolid going east on the N-122 one of the first wineries you will come to is **Abadía Retuerta**, set in an old abbey. Although geographically not in DO Ribera del Duero, it is spiritually and is worth a visit. It acts as a great indicator of the potential of the region.

The nearby town of Peñafiel is dominated by its medieval fortress. The castle has featured in numerous movies and offers spectacular views. It also houses a wine museum. The **Plaza del Coso**, ringed with balconied houses from which people traditionally watched bullfights, is a must-see as is the town's *judería* or Jewish quarter. **Bodegas Protos** on the town's main road has deep cellars under the castle and makes increasingly reliable wine. Delicious wines are

Rueda, Zona Seca

(JUAN MANUEL SANZ/ICEX)

also made by **Bodegas Pago de Carraovejas**, part owned by a famous restaurateur from Segovia.

Ribera del Duero's famous sights include **Bodegas Alejandro Fernández**, renowned for Pesquera, the region's second breakthrough wine. Winemaker Alejandro is larger than life and today also makes fabulous wines at **Condado de Haza** near Roa. Both wineries are worth visiting. His wines made headlines first when Robert Parker recommended them and later when singer Julio Iglesias acknowledged they were his favorite.

Today the mantle of fame is worn by **Bodegas Pingus**, maker of the region's most expensive wine. However, this is a very small, boutique producer

and it is almost impossible to visit. What *is* possible is to go to **Bodegas Monasterio** where winemaker Peter Sisseck (owner of Pingus) also makes some excellent, value-for-money *crianzas* and *reservas*. The winery can be easily seen from the road linking Pesquera and Valbuena.

Other wineries worth a visit are the ultra-modern **Aalto** (Mariano García is the winemaker). The beautifully designed bodega produces Aalto PS, a high-end wine that has attracted considerable critical attention.

The homely **Félix Callejo** in Sotillo adds another dimension to the region. This is a family company with a very warm and friendly atmosphere about it.

BODEGAS & MORE

SARDÓN DE DUERO
Abadía Retuerta
N-122, Km 332.5
47340 Sardón de Duero
Tel: 983 680 314
info@abadia-retuerta.com
blog.abadia-retuerta.com

VALBUENA DE DUERO
Bodegas Vega Sicilia
SA N-122, Km 322
47359 Valbuena de Duero
Tel: 983 680 147
vegasicilia@vega-sicilia.com
www.vega-sicilia.com

PEÑAFIEL
Bodegas Protos
Calle Bodegas Protos, 24-28
E-47300 Peñafiel
(Valladolid)
Tel: 983 878 011
bodega@bodegasprotos.com
www.bodegasprotos.com

Pago de Carraovejas
Camino de Carraovejas, s/n
47300 Peñafiel
Tel: 983 878 020
administracion@
pagodecarraovejas.com

WINE MUSEUM
**Museo Provincial del Vino
de Peñafiel** Castillo de
Peñafiel 47300 Peñafiel
Tel: 983 881 199
museodelvinodevalladolid.es

PESQUERA
**Bodegas Hacienda
Monasterio**
Ctra Pesquera-Valbuena s/n
47315 Pesquera de Duero
Tel: 983 484 002

**Alejandro Fernández—
Tinto Pesquera**
Calle Real, 2
47315 Pesquera de Duero
Tel: 983 870 037/39
pesquera@pesqueraafernandez.com
pesqueraafernandez.com

ROA
Condado de Haza
Carretera de la Horra s/n
09300 Roa (Burgos)
Tel: 947 525 254
info@condadodehaza.com
condadodehaza.com

QUINTANILLA
Aalto
Paraje Vallejo de Carril s/n
47360 Quintanilla
de Arriba
Tel: 902 056 337
aalto@aalto.es
www.aalto.es

SOTILLO
Bodegas Félix Callejo
Avenida del Cid, Km 16
09441 Sotillo de la Ribera
(Burgos). Tel: 947 532 312
Skype: bodegascallejo
callejo@bodegasfelixcallejo.com
bodegasfelixcallejo.com

Toro

Toro lies 67 km (42 miles) west of Valladolid and you'll need to take the A-62 or E-80 southwest past Tordesillas and then head directly west on the E-82 or A-11.

Toro wines have a long history, and it is known that Christopher Columbus headed out across the Atlantic fortified by casks of Toro wines, which he carried aboard the *Pinta*. It was while Columbus visited Queen Isabella at the castle of La Mota in Medina del Campo that he came to appreciate Toro's qualities.

Toro's glory days were relatively short lived once the capital had been moved from Valladolid to Madrid. A handful of wineries made dark, plum-scented and weightily tannic wines right up to modern times. Then Bodegas Vega Sicilia decided that the *terroir* here was too good to be ignored. This decision sparked considerable interest in the region and today Toro is rightly considered one of Spain's most exciting winemaking regions.

Vega Sicilia's investment in Toro is called Pintia, after the ancient archeological center near Peñafiel, a stone's throw from their main **Ribera del Duero** winery. There is a seductive perfume to most Toro wines, which is often accompanied by a velvety mouthfeel surrounded by mellow tannins. When young and tannic, Toro wines can be mouth-puckering and a touch aggressive, but given bottle age they are remarkable, seductive and profound.

It was while Mariano García was winemaker at Vega Sicilia that interest grew in Toro. Many observers believe it was García who launched the gold-rush. His own winery, **Maurodós**, makes San Román, some of the biggest and most outstanding wines in the region. The winery stands like a stone cube among vineyards of Tinta de Toro, the local grape variety, a clone of Tempranillo. García believes that although Tinta de Toro has plenty of character and reflects the underlying and remarkably stony *terroir* of the region, it may yet be enhanced by other introduced varieties. You can say that modern Toro's golden days are just beginning. Each year's wine

Mark Mardell of the BBC introduces viewers to Carlos Falco's renowned Marqués de Griñón vineyards at the Valdepusa estate

has been better than the previous year's and this state of affairs is likely to continue for years to come as producers come to grips with the fantastic potential of this remarkable region.

If you are downtown in Toro you'll soon find a road called Rejadorada. The name comes from an iron grill that protects a window on the wonderful old palace. There are historic wine vaults inside and a shop that sells wine made at a small winery virtually next door to Pintia and not far from Maurodós.

Their wines range from Rejadorada, to a powerful *crianza* called Novellum and is topped by a supple and gloriously balanced wine called Sango (*blood* in Esperanto).

One winery not to miss is **Bodega Numanthia Termes.** Its two wines have done a lot to illustrate the real potential of Tinta de Toro to connoisseurs. Numanthia is a deep, sensual and well-structured wine and Termanthia is a block-buster that is remarkable for its balance, compelling power and depth.

BODEGAS & MORE

PEDROSA DEL REY

Bodegas y Viñedos Maurodós
Ctra N-122, Km 412
47112 Villaester
Pedrosa del Rey
Tel: 983 784 118
sanroman@bodegasmauro.com

SAN ROMÁN DE LA HORNIJA

Bodegas y Viñedos Pintia
Carretera Morales de Toro
s/n, 47530 San Román
de la Hornija
Tel: 983 784 178
vegasicilia@vega-sicilia.com

VALDEFINJAS

Bodegas Numanthia Termes
Real s/n
49882 Valdefinjas
Tel: 980 669 147
sjorda@moet-hennessy.com

Rueda

Spaniards are not well known for their love of white wine. However, Rueda has succeeded in conquering the hearts of wine lovers in the trendy terrace bars of Madrid. **Bodegas Marqués de Riscal**, one of Rioja's oldest and most respected establishments, realized that the

Toro

traditional combination of Viura and Rioja were never going to provide world-class white wines.

Riscal had heard of Rueda and its impressive day-night temperature variations (very useful in making aromatic white wines). As a consequence they set up experimental plantations there. Initially the plan was to use Sauvignon Blanc exclusively. The discovery of the local Verdejo, a grape with a grassy, aromatic profile, added to the portfolio. Today it is Verdejo for which Rueda is principally known, from exuberant and in-your-face nettle to sophisticated and unctuous.

To get to Rueda, head for Tordesillas and take the signs to Madrid on the A-6. It's 10 km (6 miles) south of Tordesillas. You'll recognize it by its tall church bell tower, which dominates a landscape of rolling, gravelly vineyards. If you climb up the tower at night during harvest time you will see an unforgettable sight. Lights from grape picking vehicles will shine this way and that as far as the eye can see, giving the whole area an eerie, almost extraterrestrial feel.

Riscal's modern winery is just north of the town, visible as you arrive. Apart from the normal Marqués de Riscal (Verdejo with some Viura) make sure you try the Sauvignon Blanc and the Limousin (fermented in French oak).

Just off the main road in downtown Rueda you'll find **Oro de Castilla**, a family-owned winery run by Pablo del Villar. Del Villar has been experimenting with native yeasts and genetically engineered enzymes to achieve some of the smoothest and most delicate Verdejo seen yet.

Another very classy Verdejo is that produced by **Belondrade y Lurton** in La Seca. To get there you need to head out of Rueda on the VP-9902. Their barrique-fermented Verdejo is best with some bottle aging and, while more expensive than some, is worth the investment.

BODEGAS & MORE

RUEDA
Bodega de los Herederos del Marqués de Riscal
Crta N-6, Km 172.6
47490 Rueda
Tel: 983 868 029
www.marquesderiscal.es

Bodega Hermanos del Villar (Oro de Castilla)
Calle Zarcillo s/n
47490 Rueda
Tel: 983 868 904
info@orodecastilla.com

LA SECA
Bodega Belondrade y Lurton
Quinta San Diego
Camino del Puerto
47491 La Seca
Tel: 983 481 001
info@belondradeylurton.com
www.belondradeylurton.com

Cigales

Leave Valladolid going north on the A-62 or E-080 until Majada Valdetan and then follow the VP-4401 until you get to Cigales. Mariano García has described the *terroir* in Cigales as some of the best in Spain. The vineyards here overlook the Duero Valley and the setting of Valladolid. The first winery on this route is **La Legua**, founded by Valladolid psychiatrist Emeterio Fernández. It all began as a hobby to take his mind off the demanding nature of his work but has ended up being one of the standard-bearers of the region. Make sure you try La Legua's Capricho, a

small-production wine of outstanding quality.
  Bodega Valdelosfrailes came into being when Carlos Moro, then responsible for the impressive Matarromera Group, chose to invest in Cigales rather than trendy Ribera del Duero or Toro. The bodega's Pago del las Costanas is a reference in quality red winemaking.

BODEGAS & MORE

La Legua
Ctra Cigales Km 1
47194 Fuensaldaña
Tel: 983 583 244
lalegua@lalegua.com
www.lalegua.com

Bodega Valdelosfrailes
Ctra Quintanilla 5
47359 Olivares de Duero
Tel: 983 660 454
www.matarromera.es

The mountains of Segovia

The route from Valladolid to Madrid is dotted with many beautiful old towns famed for their delicious cuisine. Old-style wood ovens are used gently to bake succulent lamb dishes redolent of woodsmoke and, most aromatic of all, dried vine cuttings known as *sarmientos*. The area is of great beauty, with towns of lovely old stone houses, most of which have been restored by wealthy Madrid dwellers as weekend retreats. Still, there is a hint of old Spain lingering here.

Medina del Campo

Just south of Tordesillas you'll find Medina del Campo with its impressive La Mota castle where Queen Isabella, who married Ferdinand of Aragón and thus united Spain, died in 1504. Then take the small C-112 that leads east from Medina towards Sepúlveda.

Sepúlveda and Riaza

The walled town of Cuéllar on the CL-601 is well worth a visit on the way south. However, a must-see is the town of Sepúlveda, which is 110 km (68 miles) south of Medina del Campo. Sepúlveda is a picturesque old stone town, just to the east of the **Las Hoces del Río Duratón** nature reserve. During lunchtime you'll find the whole area perfumed with the scent of delicious food being prepared. If you can, pay a visit to the artificial lake in the nature reserve early in the morning. As the sun's rays heat up the day, vultures will take to the air on rising thermals from cliff-side roosts, a rare and special sight.

An alternative to Sepúlveda is Riaza on the other side of the N-1. City weekenders have not quite spoiled its ancient charm with their vacation homes. Its center remains reasonably unspoiled with a circular plaza ringed by an arcade of quaint bars and cafés. The plaza acts as a bullring during the town's annual fiesta.

Further along the N-1 turn west on to the N-110 to Segovia. Follow the signs to the charming old town of **Pedraza de la Sierra** with its old houses and cobbled streets, an absolute must.

Segovia

Segovia is one of Spain's most magnificent cities, and well worth spending time in. Among its many sights is one of the finest Roman aqueducts in Europe; a beautifully preserved **Alcázar** (from which Isabella and Ferdi-

(HAROLD HECKLE)

Vega Sicilia, perhaps Spain's most revered winery, has made top wines since 1864; the extraordinary Único is its flagship wine

nand planned and then embarked on the reunification of Spain and the expulsion of the Islamic kingdoms); and one of the most beautiful old quarters in the peninsula.

On the way in to the old walled city you'll come across an odd sight—a monument to a chef slicing roast suckling pig on a plate. This is a tribute to one of the region's most famous dishes, *cochinillo asado*. The secret of the dish is that the animal is killed when only three weeks old and then roasted slowly in a large oven for maximum succulence.

Make sure you try the version from the **Mesón de Cándido**, near the aqueduct. All around the main square, next to the imposing cathedral and the wonderful old theater, you'll find a fantastic array of bars and restaurants. As the sun sets people throng here to converse, enjoy a beverage and share tapas before heading off for dinner.

On your way to Madrid make sure you visit the royal palace and monastery of **El Escorial**. Once the seat of power of what was then the largest empire the world had ever known, it was Phillip II's operational headquarters. Try and see the royal library—it is truly unforgettable. El Escorial is also an excellent place for lunch.

FOR FURTHER
INFORMATION
Segovia Tourist Office
Plaza Mayor, 9
40001 Segovia
Tel: 921 466 070
info@turismodesegovia.com
www.segoviaturismo.es

The gastronomy of Castile

Winter stews are a feature of Castile's cuisine, and paprika (called *pimenton*), spiced chorizo sausages (try those from León) and *morcilla* (blood sausage or black pudding), impart flavor and aroma to the region's great stews such as *Cachelada* and *Ropa Vieja* (literally "old clothes" as it was often made from yesterday's leftovers). You may find meat combined with beans and fried egg in both.

The **hornos de asar**

Castile has always been famous for its roasting ovens, or *hornos de asar*. Heated with pine wood, vine shoots or pungent eucalyptus, these are made with bricks or mud in a conical shape and are used to bake bread or roast meat. Try the bread, tender lamb, goat or suckling pig. Roast meats such as lamb (*cordero*), suckling pig (*cochinillo*) and kid (*cabrito*) are central to Castile's understanding of a good lunch. Two restaurants to try are **Mesón de Cándido,** the quintessential restaurant for suckling pig, and **José María**. The latter is is one of the most popular restaurants in Segovia, where you can enjoy delicious lamb chops, suckling pig or oven-baked lamb. Do try the restaurant's own Ribera del Duero wine, Pago de Carraovejas.

The oven-baked breads of Castile add an extra dimension to any meal. Spaniards cannot conceive of a meal without bread and expect to be served aromatic bread of different shapes and consistency without being asked.

Fish dishes

Modern refrigerated transportation has enabled Spain to become a paradise for fish lovers even when far from the coast. Most fish is sea-fresh with one notable exception. Cod is almost always salted. Although it is de-salted

Nava de Rey, Ribera del Duero

before cooking it retains a hint of salinity, which lovers of fresh cod may find irritating. River trout can be excellent in León and Segovia. Generally fish is tampered with very little in the kitchen: typically it will be grilled or oven baked.

Food specialties

Spanish salt-cured ham is one of the ultimate delicacies of Iberian cuisine. Most bars or restaurants will have a leg of ham, which is thinly sliced into pieces that are roughly two inches square. These are then delicately placed on a dish for you to pick up with your fingers. The best ham is called *Iberico de bellota* (from a type of pig called the Iberico, which has been allowed to range free and is fed on acorns for added flavor). You should also try *Jamón Serrano* (ham from pigs reared on mountain ranges like the Alpujarras in Andalusia). When away from home Spaniards dream about eating *jamón*.

Another dish you will be expected to eat with your fingers is *chuletas de cordero* (lamb chops). Castile lamb is famous for its gentle flavor, usually enhanced by woodsmoke and sometimes served with baked green or red peppers.

Ever since the expulsion of Muslims and Jews from the peninsula, rearing pigs for pork has played an important part in the life of rural Spain. Families get together once a year to slaughter animals (*la matanza*) and prepare ham and

pork sausages (*chorizo*).

Menestra a la Palentina is a vegetable stew, best in late summer when the vegetables are young and tender. As Spaniards are notoriously non-vegetarian, you may find slices of chicken and bacon are added to artichokes, zucchini, peas, potatoes and broad beans to make a wonderful stew that is slow-cooked in white wine.

Perdices a la Segoviana This is a dish based on partridge, small game typical of central Spain. Partridges are baked in earthenware dishes alongside vegetables. Another stew, *Ropa Vieja* is cooked chicken, pork, beef or a mixture of meats with beans, chickpeas and a fried sauce made of onions, peppers and eggplant.

Rape Castellano is monkfish in a thick sauce of onions, pine nuts, eggs and, if you are lucky, succulent and tangy clams.

Fiestas

Castile has many fiestas, and every town celebrates its patron saint with an annual bash. Bulls often take pride of place in these events, but be warned, though they are very colorful, you need a strong stomach for some of them. The *Toro de la Vega* fiesta in Tordesillas is said to have been started by Joanna the Mad, who watched it from Santa Clara. A bull is released in the town's central square and is then chased out on to the plain (*Vega*) where it is killed by men on horseback.

WHERE TO STAY AND EAT

Segovia

José María
Cronista Lecea, 11
40001 Segovia
Tel: 921 461 111
reservas@rtejosemaria.es
www.rtejosemaria.com (R)

Mesón de Cándido
Azoquejo, 5
40001 Segovia
Tel: 921 425 911
candido@mesondecandido.es
www.mesondecandido.es (R)

Sepúlveda

Figón Zute el Mayor
Calle Lope Tablada, 6, or
its sister restaurant **Figón**

de Tinín Calle Alfonso VI,
40300 Sepúlveda
Tel: 921 540 165
     921 540 440
zutemayor@figondetinin.com
www.figondetinin.com (R)

Tordesillas

Parador de Tordesillas
Carretera Salamanca 5
47100 Tordesillas
Tel: 983 770 051
www.parador.es (H)

Valladolid

AC Palacio De Santa Ana
Calle Santa Ana s/n
Arroyo de la Encomienda

Old bush vines of Tinta de Toro growing on sandy soils
near San Román de Hornija, Toro

47195 Valladolid
Tel: 983 409 920
psantaana@ac-hotels.com
www.ac-hotels.com (H/R)

Hotel Imperial
Calle del Peso, 4
47001 Valladolid
Tel: 983 330 300
www.himperial.com

Restaurante mil vinos
Plaza Martí y Monsó
esquina Calle Comedias
47001 Valladolid
Tel: 983 344 336

Vinotinto Parrilla
Calle Campanas 4
47001 Valladolid
Tel: 983 342 291
A charcoal grill to dream

about. As its name suggests,
red wine goes best with the
excellent grilled meats
on offer. (R)

Mesón La Fragua
Paseo de Zorrilla 10
47080 Valladolid
Tel: 983 338 785
A traditional restaurant
with good quality local
cuisine.

Parrilla de San Lorenzo
Calle Pedro Niño 1
47001 Valladolid
Tel: 983 335 088
Housed in a national
monument, the Royal
Monastery of San
Bernardo. (R)

(HAROLD HECK-E)

THE SOUTHEAST
MURCIA

I N THE 1970S AND 80S, self-protective French producers used to refer to Spanish wine as "hot country wine," implying an unspoken superiority to their supposedly cool climate alternatives. Then came the "fruit bomb" revolution. It was in 1990 that Agapito Rico, a fun-loving businessman from the region of Murcia, decided to act on a hunch. Since his childhood he had seen wines from his native region departing in massive quantities aboard trains and tankers to destinations that included Rioja as well as, yes, France. What was it, he wondered, that such famous vinicultural regions came looking for in the wines of Murcia? "They come for the color and alcoholic strength their northern climates cannot give them," his elders told Rico. Yet he suspected there was more to it than that. Acting on his intuition, he sparked a transformation that has won praise from experts everywhere.

The region of Murcia is located halfway between Valencia to the north and Almería to the south. The A-7 (or AP-7) links all three capital cities bearing the same names as their regions. There are good airports to all three. Murcia is blessed with three great wine denominations: Bullas, Jumilla and Yecla. All three are situated within valleys, environments that contain the best meteorological conditions, called microclimates, for vine cultivation.

Something about the valleys of Murcia exudes history. They evoke and almost seem to yearn for a time long gone by. Ancient Moorish castles rest atop strategically important promontories and even the food is redolent of a lost civilization. Water is scarce here, and agriculture relies on the oldest science of irrigation, perfected by the Moors. Though modern drip irrigation keeps many vineyards healthy, some valleys retain techniques imported from

« Monastrell vines growing on chalky soil in the Carche Valley, Murcia

THE SOUTHEAST–MURCIA

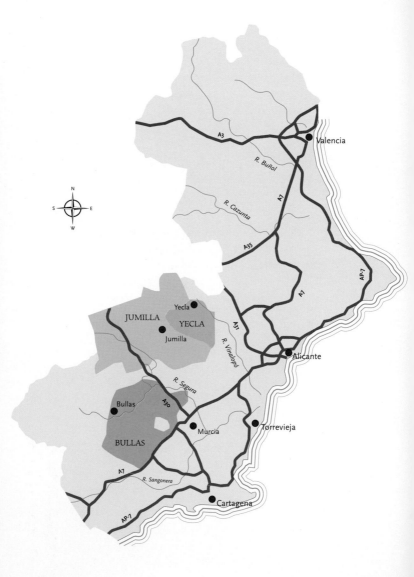

ancient Syria. Long-suffering mules used to plod endlessly around stone-built *saquiyas*, mechanisms that pumped water from deep wells. The concept gave rise to *acequias*, irrigation ditches, that are still used. Only the mules have given way to gasoline pumps. It is easy to see how some Moorish words have remained in the language through the ages: *aljibe* (water tank or cistern) and *noria* (water wheel).

A key component: Monastrell

The Monastrell grape variety reigns supreme in Murcia. When Rico sensed there was something special in the wines of the area, he wasn't wrong. The local climate has enabled Monastrell to evolve into a perfectly adapted grape. Few grapes manage to convey a sense of place better than Monastrell. There are no accurate records of when it was introduced here but it was a long time ago, around the time almond trees were first imported.

Over the last 20 years wine experts have found similarities between Monastrell and two successful grape varieties from further north: Mourvèdre in France and Graciano in Rioja. Mourvèdre contributes spicy, memorable qualities to Châteauneuf-du-Pape and Bandol in France's Rhône Valley.

Riojanos say Graciano "lends grace" to their wines. Both regions share a common difficulty, however, Graciano is slow to ripen. This problem simply doesn't exist in Murcia.

The wine regions of Murcia

Jumilla

Thanks to Rico's pioneering work at his property in the El Carche Valley, named after the valley's dominant mountain, Jumilla spurred Murcia's change to modern winemaking. Murcia's vineyards are full of Monastrell and, as with so many regions of Spain, wines from here were first exported to France in the wake of phylloxera.

Agapito Rico

Rico knew there was something missing in order to take Murcian wines a step further. His hunch was that greater complexity, both aromatic and flavor-related, could yield better results. Rico chose Cabernet Sauvignon. Famous for its connections with Bordeaux, this added red berry aromas to the traditional fleshy plums of Murcian wines. As time went by, however, it became clear that Cabernet's distinctive aromatic qualities tended to become too bright, almost acetaldehyde tinged, in Murcia's hot growing conditions. The added complexity was offset by aromatic imbalances.

Rico then stumbled across the real key to success, Syrah. Today Cabernet has given way to more Monastrell planting along with some Syrah. The two grapes combine spectacularly well. Rico has sold his interest in the winery, and it now exists as **Bodegas Carchelo**. Once harvested, the varieties are vinified separately before winemaker Joaquín Gálvez decides each wine's final blend. Carchelo Joven is full of rich fruit, prunes and plums. Carchelo Crianza is bigger, remarkably balanced, rich and spicy. Varietal Syrah Altico (four months in oak) and Canalizo (18 months in oak) reveal the success this Rhône variety has had in Murcia.

Bodega Casa de la Ermita

Pedro José Martínez, son of growers in the El Carche valley, joined forces with Marcial Martínez, who had worked with Agapito Rico, to launch **Bodega La Ermita** in 1999. "The project was begun from zero," says export director Lorenzo Baños, "and we now sell wine to 35 countries." Right from the beginning there were plans to allow for tourism, with a staff member appointed specifically to look after visitors. In the middle of La Ermita's vineyards you'll find a preserved underground cave once used as a dwelling. "All around Murcia little caves were used by farmers," explains Baños. "You'll even find some in the old quarters of towns." Inside the little hermitage, which gives the winery its

(HAROLD HECKLE)

Pepa Fernández is part-owner of Bodegas Balcona in Bullas, where she makes organic wines of great depth and character

name, there are several chambers: living quarters, a place for animals, an oven to bake bread and a fireplace to roast dinners, with a chimney rising to the surface. Esparto grass mats once used to collect olives are still visible, as are grass cheese moulds, all painstakingly preserved.

Try the Petit Verdot from vines imported in 2001. Casa de la Ermita is 50 percent Monastrell, 15 percent Tempranillo, 15 percent Cabernet Sauvignon: the final 20 percent is a blend of Merlot and Syrah. Casa de la Ermita Crianza adds 4 percent Petit Verdot to 40 percent each of Monastrell and Tempranillo plus 16 percent of Cabernet Sauvignon.

Finca Luzón

Luzón began making bulk wine in 1916 and by the mid 1990s it was being exported to Russia. The profits were invested in stainless steel. Today winemaker Luis Sánchez makes Finca Luzón from 65 percent Monastrell with 35 percent Syrah. Altos de Luzón blends old block Monastrell with Tempranillo and Cabernet (50-25-25). Blockbuster Alma de Luzón tops its list.

Casa Castillo

At Kilometer 15.7 on the C-3213 road from Jumilla to Hellín you'll come across an idyllic country setting, the location of a winery called **Bodega Julia Roch e Hijos** on their Finca Casa Castillo estate. Winemaker José María Vicente cultivates 200 hectares of vines and olives (mainly Picual variety). This region's low rainfall and an inability to irrigate "simply because there isn't any water around to draw on," govern Vicente's style of what he calls extreme viticulture.

The soil is far stonier than most in Murcia, a region already notable for rocky topsoil. This characteristic prompted Vicente to plant Syrah vines brought from Hermitage in the Rhône. There are 24 hectares of very stony land planted with Syrah. Of around 400,000 bottles produced, around half are vineyard- or *terroir-* specific, and of those, 70,000 bottles are of special Syrah grown on the stony Val Tosca vineyard. Still, Monastrell remains the winery's main output. "I used to make classic-style Monastrell: now I like to make wine which is more friendly, more like those from southern France, with ripe tannins and good acidity," explains Vicente.

Look for joyful Valtosca wines with nine months in oak, 60 percent of which is new. Pie Franco spends 18 months in barrel and is harvested from very old block

(HAROLD HECKLE)

The immaculately clean and airy fermentation hall at Casa la Ermita in Jumilla

Monastrell vines grown ungrafted on stony soils. The wine has a controlled, tight-knit aroma that you simply know is going to improve after a year or two in bottle. However, Vicente warns against aging: "If you want to enjoy Mediterranean wine in all its fullness then drink it immediately."

Bodegas El Nido

The standout winery of Jumilla is also one of its exceptions. Rather than opt for Syrah, it still vinifies Cabernet Sauvignon. Australian winemaker Chris Ringland of Barossa Valley fame has managed to create two absolutely fantastic wines in Clio and blockbuster El Nido. Neither wine comes cheap, and it will probably be next to impossible to visit this small winery, but at the very least you have to try them, even if it is at a restaurant.

Clio is 30 percent Cabernet Sauvignon and 70 percent Monastrell (from 60-year-old vines) that underwent malolactic fermentation in new oak followed by 26 months' aging in new French and American barriques. El Nido comes from 30-year-old Cabernet

Sauvignon (70 percent) and 60-year-old Monastrell (30 percent), and was aged 26 months in new French and American oak barrels after malolactic fermentation.

FOR FURTHER INFORMATION

DO Jumilla
Calle San Roque 15
30520 Jumilla
Tel: 968 781 761
info@vinosdejumilla.org
www.vinosdejumilla.org

BODEGAS & MORE

Bodegas Carchelo Paraje
Calle Casas de la Hoya s/n
Apdo de Correos nº 36
30520 Jumilla
Tel: 968 435 137
administracion@carchelo.com

Bodegas Casa de la Ermita
Avda de la Asunción
42 - Bajo, Apdo de Correos
nº 289, 30520 Jumilla
Tel: 968 783 035
bodega@casadelaermita.com
www.casadelaermita.com

Bodegas Luzón
Ctra Jumilla-Calasparra
Km 3.1, Apdo de Correos
nº 92, 30520 Jumilla
Tel: 968 784 135
info@bodegasluzon.com
www.bodegasluzon.com

Casa Castillo
Ctra Héllin-Jumilla Km
15.7, Apdo de Correos nº 3
30520 Jumilla
Tel: 968 781 691
info@casacastillo.es
www.casacastillo.es

Bodegas El Nido
Portillo de la Glorieta nº 7
bajo, Apartado de correos
nº 2, 30520 Jumilla
Tel: 629 261 379
info@bodegaselnido.com
www.bodegaselnido.com

Harvest festival

Every year Jumilla sets aside
seven days in August to
celebrate the **Fiesta de la
Vendimia**, or harvest festival. People dress as *huertano*
peasants and participate
in, among other things, an
all-out wine battle similar
to one held every June in
Haro, Rioja. Wine is thrown
everywhere, like at an
age-old Bacchanalian feast.
Officials calculated around

100,000 people participate.
Harvest time in Murcia lasts
around two months. First
to be picked are the white
grapes, usually led by Chardonnay, then Tempranillo,
Merlot, Monastrell and
finally Petit Verdot.

Bullas

The Aceniche Valley is an
ecological dream devoid of
telegraph poles and paved
roads, a reminder of how
the countryside looked a
couple of centuries ago.
Within this natural envi-
ronment, Pepa Fernández
of **Bodegas Balcona** and
her family cultivate the
grapes that make Partal
wines. The first modern
style wines were made in
1998. Winemaker José
Manuel Barnuevo has skill-
fully combined French and
American oak to achieve
highly aromatic, deeply
textured wines. Monastrell
packs huge amounts of

Cheese molds, Jumilla

(HAROLD HECKLE)

prune-led fruit. The soil, or *terroir*, here clearly leaves an imprint. Syrah grown on the ferruginous clay soils of the region outstrips Cabernet Sauvignon. Partal I is made from un-irrigated grapes. Casa de la Cruz is typical of "hot country" wines, packing loads of fruit. "With only 800 bottles made, I wonder how many people will get to see this wine," says Fernández.

BODEGAS & MORE

DO Bullas website:
www.bullas.es

Bodega Balcona
Democracia N⁰ 7
30180 Bullas
Tel: 968 652 891
bodegabalcona@larural.es
www.partal-vinos.com

Yecla

Bodegas Castaño is, by any standards, a major winery. Situated next to the bullring in the picturesque, furniture-making town of Yecla (population 30,000), it's impossible to miss due to its size. Ninety percent of Castaño's production is exported to the USA, Germany and the UK.

Yet, despite the juggernaut size of his operation, winemaker Marcelino López is adaptable enough to listen carefully to his customers and even make wines tailored to the tastes of important buyers and importers. Within Spain, for example, López vinifies some special wines for wine connoisseur and retailer Quim Vila (owner of Vila Viniteca wine shop in Barcelona). Vila buys, among other specialties, a wine made principally from the normally oxidative and very fussy Garnacha Tintorera (known as Alicante Bouschet in France and southern Portugal).

Castaño's flagship wine is Hécula, a brand launched in 1992 that has now reached annual production of 600,000 bottles. Other wines worth exploring include Castaño Colección made from 80 percent Monastrell and 20 percent Cabernet Sauvignon, aged 14 months in oak. Yecla's *terroir* produces wines with aromas that emerge seductively. If you order from Vila Viniteca (which has an excellent mail order service) try Viña al lado de la casa from Monastrell, Cabernet Sauvignon and Syrah, with around a year in oak. Casa Cisca is a small-production wine (named after family grandmother Francisca) made from very old vine Monastrell.

BODEGAS & MORE

DO Yecla
Calle Poeta Francisco
A Jiménez s/n
Polígono URBAYECLA II
30510 Yecla
Tel: 968 792 352
info@yeclavino.com
www.yeclavino.com

Bodegas Castaño
Ctra Fuentealamo 3
30510 Yecla
Tel: 968 791 115
info@bodegascastano.com
www.bodegascastano.com

Eating in Murcia

Hotel SG is a clean modern hotel a short walk from Bullas' town center. It has a steady if traditional menu and a reasonable wine list—although be warned, people around here seem to like white wine more mature than crisp and fresh. Ask for recent vintages of white. **Cafetería-Burger Bar** Arlequín, also in Bullas, has a spectacular array of tapas, beautifully presented, as well as a good selection of wines and beers.

A cozy hotel situated outside the city of Jumilla, **Hotel Casa Luzón** has wonderful vineyard views and a superb restaurant that specializes in local dishes such as fried goat's cheese with tomato sauce and the unique *gazpacho jumillano*, a dish redolent of Jumilla's rich historical past.

Restaurante El Sordo, in the achingly beautiful mountain village of Ricote, is *the* place to eat while on wine tours in Murcia. Talented chef and serious wine lover Jesús Ortega López specializes in game, but has an impressive menu and jaw-dropping wine list. Mind you, mature whites can prevail here too. Even a Château d'Yquem 1955 when last visited!

In Yecla, **Cafetería El Tapeo** owner Agustín Díaz Abellán presents attractive tapas and flavorsome menus at this busy and hard-working cafe-restaurant. **Hotel La Paz** is a surprisingly modern, clean and agreeable hotel on Yecla's main approach road. Its in-house restaurant, **Ródenas**, has an attractive menu.

WHERE TO STAY AND EAT

Bullas

Hotel SG
General Antonio
Sanchez 38
30180 Bullas
Tel/fax 902 220 203 (I I/R)

**Cafetería-Burger
Bar Arlequín**
Raimundo Muñoz 9
30180 Bullas
Tel: 968 654 055

Jumilla

Hotel Casa Luzón
Carretera Jumilla-Ontur
Km 17, 30520 Jumilla
Tel: 968 780 206
Fax 968 781 911

Bar-Restaurante Venecia
Dr. Fleming, 7
30520 Jumilla
Tel: 968 783 298

Ricote

Restaurante El Sordo
Alharbona s/n
30610 Ricote
Tel: 968 697 209
elsordo@e-taller.net

Yecla

Cafetería El Tapeo
Avenida Feria s/n
30510 Yecla

Hotel La Paz
Avenida La Paz 180
30510 Yecla
Tel: 968 751 350
Fax 968 753 257
info@lapaz-hoTel.com
www.lapaz-hoTel.com

Dovecote, Yecla

(HARO_D HECKLE)

ANDALUSIA

THE NAME ANDALUSIA (Andalucía in Spanish) says it all. Derived directly from the Arabic original Al-Andalus, the name the Moors gave to their kingdom in the south of Spain, it is imbued with both the mystery of a kingdom vanished and the magic of its modern vitality. It was not until 1492 that the last caliphate of Al-Andalus, that of Granada, fell to the *Reconquista* (Reconquest) of Spain by the northern Catholic kings.

To this day reminders of an Arab and Berber past linger with remarkable potency. So strong is the influence that even in the depths of the modern Costa del Sol with all its horrors of mass tourism you can still see unmistakable traces. There are old Moorish castles, fortresses and watchtowers all along the Mediterranean coast. There is something magical about this great, sprawling southern region. If you can avoid the tourist traps, driving around Andalusia can be a truly memorable experience—one of the best in Europe.

Some precautions will help you enjoy wine in this historic land. Andalusia is a region of potent *vinos generosos*, fortified wines, as well as brandies and wonderfully aromatic olive oils. Your head and liver can take a serious pounding if you don't watch out. Add to this summer temperatures that can (and often do) exceed 40°C (104°F) and you can see how you might end up flattened. I have seen almost unbelievable temperatures recorded in midsummer days.

My advice is always to ensure that you carry plenty of water in your car and drink it constantly while enjoying wines and food. And always drink some before going to bed.

Driving south from Madrid on the new Carretera de Andalucía you go through Valdepeñas, then Jaén with its impressive Parador that used to be a Moorish fort, heading for the small town of Bailén. At this point you can decide

《 Detail in a Mudejar chapel in Córdoba, Andalusia, shows the fusion of Islamic and Spanish motifs

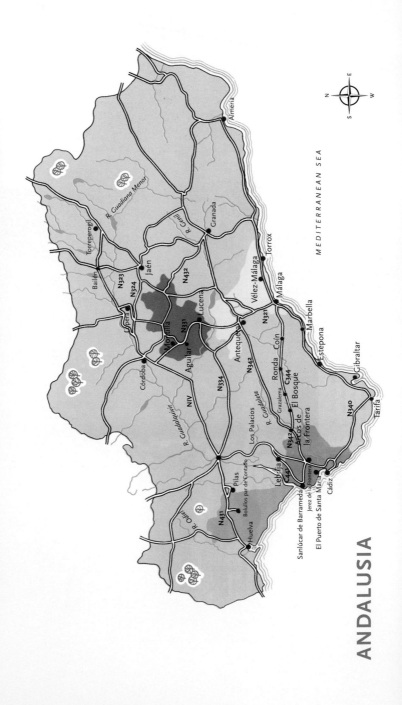

MEDITERRANEAN SEA

Almería

Granada

Torrox

Vélez-Málaga

Málaga

Marbella

Estepona

Gibraltar

Tarifa

N340

R. Guadiana Menor

R. Genil

Torreperogil

Jaén

N432

Bailén

N323

N324

Úbeda

Lucena

Moriles

N331

Aguilar

Antequera

N342

Ronda

Coín

N321

C344

El Bosque

Grazalema

Córdoba

NIV

N334

R. Guadalete

Los Palacios

Arcos de la Frontera

N342

N340

R. Guadalquivir

Lebrija

Jerez de la Frontera

Cádiz

Pilas

Bollullos par de Contado

Sanlúcar de Barrameda

El Puerto de Santa María

N431

Huelva

R. Odiel

N E S W

ANDALUSIA

which direction to take. Directly south lies the magic of Granada. Head west and you'll be in wine country with Córdoba, the former Moorish capital of Al-Andalus, as your destination.

The wine region of Montilla lies south of Córdoba, reachable on the N-331. Carry on westward from Córdoba and you head for sherry country. South and beyond Montilla you will descend on to the Mediterranean coast and Málaga, another ancient and intriguing wine region.

Córdoba

The first stop of your Andalusian wine tour should be the justly famous city of Córdoba. Apart from being the historic capital of the former Moorish kingdom of Al-Andalus, it had previously been the capital of the Roman province of Baetica. Córdoba has outstanding monuments to its historic past.

In the center of town lies the **Mezquita**, or mosque, once the largest building in the world after the pyramids. Following the Reconquista this amazing building was turned, rather unimaginatively, into a drab cathedral. Next to it, in the center of town, is a Roman bridge that crosses the Guadalquivir River. The nearby **Alcázar**, or fort, has splendid gardens.

Five kilometers (3 miles) west of Córdoba if you turn north off the A-431 you'll come across what remains of **Medina Azahara**—one of the largest country palaces ever built, the Versailles of its time.

One could not hope for a better introduction to this great southern province.

The Judería of Córdoba

For a wine and food enthusiast this is an excellent place to begin a local apprenticeship. The *Judería* or old Jewish quarter is a maze of narrow alleys that cut through whitewashed houses. Once a year in May, this district bursts into bloom during the **Fiesta de los Patios Córdobeses**, when the inhabitants decorate their courtyards, balconies and squares with potted plants in bloom (geraniums predominate). A soulful, austere variant of flamenco music typifies Córdoba. There is a wealth of small, hidden bars and restaurants where chilled Montilla Fino is served with a wide variety of tapas.

An evening spent prowling these alleys from bar to bar, much as Spaniards themselves do, can be a thoroughly enjoyable experience. Remember to drink plenty of water while you are at it to spare the worst excesses the following morning. For food enthusiasts, there are plenty of sophisticated restaurants to choose from.

Córdoba's sherry connection

The principal wine of Córdoba is Montilla, produced just to the south of the city in and around the towns of Montilla, Moriles and Aguilar de la Frontera. The style is very similar to sherry, a resemblance that has caused local producers considerable heartache, as it is nowhere near as famous nor as sought after. Up until 1944, when the Denomination was first established, much of the region's wine was sold to the great sherry houses of Jerez where it was, quite legally, pumped into their solera systems and eventually sold as sherry. Even today some forms of Jerez, like the sweet Pedro Ximénez (PX for short), are sourced mainly if not exclusively from Montilla-Moriles.

It is now illegal for non-PX wine from Montilla-Moriles to be sold as sherry and Montilla producers have had to stand on their own feet. Dispelling the myth that their wines are a cheap alternative to sherry has been a hard task. Producers have invested wisely, raised the quality of their wines and established a following among drinkers who prefer lower alcoholic strengths to those of sherry. Fino *en rama* from Montilla can be quite a revelation, and Amontillados (which means "in the manner of Montilla") from the area simply must be tried.

The DO Montilla-Moriles embraces some 10,082 hectares (25,000 acres) of vineyards. Of these, some 2900 hectares (about 7200 acres) of *albariza* or *albero* soil have been designated as *Zona Superior*, which usually produce dry or Fino wines. The *arenas* or *ruedo* soils, composed mostly of sand with clay and limestone, usually make heavier Oloroso wines.

(HAROLD HECKLE)

A winery worker using a *venencia* pours a glass of very old Palo Cortado
sherry at Bodegas Osborne, Jerez

Bar Juan Peron in Córdoba, Andalusia. A must-visit tapas bar

Finos are normally made from the free-run must from the first pressing, while Olorosos are made from a second pressing. Pedro Ximénez is the principal grape variety with smaller quantities of Layrén (Airén), Baladí and Torrontés.

Trying to park a car in Córdoba is inevitably difficult, as in so many Spanish cities designed centuries before the car was invented. For this reason staying just outside town is worth considering.

FOR FURTHER
INFORMATION
Parador Avda de
la Arruzafa, 37
14012 Córdoba
Tel: 957 275 900
cordoba@parador.es
www.parador.es
A modern-style building
overlooking the city from a
neighboring hill.

Montilla

Sherry and Montilla
share many similarities.
Both have a basic range of
styles—Fino, Amontillado,

Oloroso, Cream and Pedro Ximénez. Despite some subtle differences, their production processes are broadly similar.

In Montilla, after the wine's first fermentation, it is transferred into *tinajas*, earthenware containers with pointed bases, which are stuck into the earth. After a second fermentation, the flor, a thick layer of yeasts that covers the top of the *tinaja*, begins to develop. The flor slows oxidation and, according to its attributes, enables winemakers to classify

the wines. After two years in butt, the wine is put through the solera system, a process that Montilla claims to have pioneered.

The differences

Sherry and Montilla have significant differences. Few would claim that Montilla achieves the intensity and complexity of great sherry, but Montilla does have its advantages. It is made principally from the Pedro Ximénez grape, a variety that in the blistering heat of the Córdoba summer produces wines with elevated alcoholic strength. Consequently, dry Montilla is never fortified and Oloroso only when it has insufficient natural strength. Montilla, therefore, is usually lighter and more natural than sherry. In recent years local bodegas have also started to make lighter, fruitier table wines called *jóvenes afrutados,* which are modern in style, pleasant and fruit-driven.

The town of Montilla

Montilla is 45 km (28 miles) due south of Córdoba along the NIV and then the smaller N-331, which winds its way through undulating countryside. Around the town, the vineyards planted on the famous *albariza* soils that have a high chalk content are grayish-white in color with yellow streaks and produce the best wines. The town itself is typically Andalusian, with the wilting heat of the sun reflected from the white walls of the houses, and colorful flowerpots hung from the windows. Travellers are advised to stay in Córdoba for the food and nightlife, though Montilla has reasonable accommodation, and there are good restaurants. Montilla is also

(CHRISTINE CLARK)

The Andalusian School of Equestrian Art in Jerez

the home of most of the largest and most important companies in the DO.

The bodegas

A couple of decades ago, there were over 20 export-quality bodegas in the Montilla DO. Changing habits and a trend towards lighter wines have taken their toll. Now there are barely ten left. One of Spain's flagship wineries is **Alvear**, founded in Montilla by Diego de Alvear y Escalera in 1729. There is no better place to see Montilla's versatility at work than in this stately and monumental bodega.

An ideal entry point into the chameleon quality of Pedro Ximénez is Alvear's Marqués de la Sierra 2002. This is a white wine that blends early-picked PX with small amounts of Riesling, Chardonnay and Sauvignon Blanc. The result is a pleasantly surprising, refreshingly modern *blanco*. It carries subtly floral hints with a clean nose and enough structure to ensure an enjoyable summer experience.

A short drive out of Montilla, at Aguilar de la Frontera, **Toro Albalá**, much like Alvear and Perez Barquero, welcomes visitors (phone first). Antonio Sanchez Romero, owner and winemaker, is a wine paraphernalia collector and as his bodega is built in what used to be an electric plant, the local expression "being electrocuted" means that someone has had a drink too many. Their *Fino en rama* is called Eléctrico. These wines hail from Moriles, which some claim is the best region because it develops the best flor.

Montilla is a compact, agreeable town to visit, especially during Holy Week. You can drive down from Córdoba in the morning, visit a winery or two and have lunch. Then in the afternoon you can visit the historic mansion **Casa del Inca Garcilaso** with its archives and library linked to Peru, one of Spain's wealthiest former South American colonies.

BODEGAS & MORE

Alvear SA
María Auxiliadora, 1
14550 Montilla
Tel: 957 650 100/
    957 652 939
info@alvear.es
www.alvear.es

Toro Albalá
Avda Antonio Sánchez 1
14920 Aguilar de la Frontera
Tel: 957 660 046
r.sanchez@toroalbala.com
www.toroalbala.com

Pérez Barquero
Avda de Andalucia, 27
14550 Montilla
Tel: 957 650 500
info@perezbarquero.com
www.perezbarquero.com

Montilla styles

These are the basic
Montilla styles:

Fino (Pale Dry) Pale in
color, light and dry. Less
salty than sherry (try *fino
en rama*).

Amontillado (softer), a
Fino that has been left
in cask until its color has
turned to amber. Dry and
fuller-bodied than Fino.

Palo Cortado A Fino with
some Oloroso blended in.
Very rare.

Oloroso Brown in color,
medium or sometimes
with a hint of sweetness.

Pale Cream A Fino that
has been sweetened.
Golden in color, full-

bodied, pungent with a
hint of dryness.

Cream A sweetened
Oloroso. Dark and richly
sweet.

Pedro Ximénez Made from
grapes that have been
dried in the sun. Raisiny,
almost black and extremely
sweet.

Alcohol in all these styles
ranges from 14 to 22 percent
by volume.

In the US/UK the terms
Fino and Amontillado are
reserved for sherry only:
Pale Dry and Medium are
used for the same styles of
Montilla.

Málaga

From Montilla the N-331
leads south across the very
heart of Andalusia. This is
a road from which you can
appreciate the full majesty
of the landscape of rolling
hills decorated by beautiful *cortijos* (farmhouses) and
olive groves.

Antequera, some 60 km
(38 miles) from Mon-
tilla, justifies a short stop.
Visit its old castle with its
gardens and views over the
great plain of Antequera,
500 m (1600 ft) above sea

(HAROLD HECKLE)

Palomino and Moscatel grape vines criss-cross the Andalusian landscape at Montilla, south of Córdoba

level Many of the vineyards used in the production of Málaga wine are planted around here. Then continue on to the N-321, and a slow descent down the southern slopes of the western Sierra de Almijara to the port city of Málaga.

The city of Málaga

Málaga is still, in my eyes, an unspoiled Spanish city of splendid gardens and tree-lined avenues overlooked by the imposing Alcazaba fortress. It has excellent restaurants and hotels and, mercifully, most tourists who land at its airport do not even bother to visit it.

Though Málaga is always a lively city, it is best visited at Eastertime when there are magnificent religious processions and the Spanish Foreign Legion holds a parade near the port. In the eastern part of the city is the **El Palo** district with an abundance of restaurants on the beach serving fish freshly caught in the bay in the morning.

To the west is the **Costa del Sol** and its tourist traps but towns like **Benalmadena** and **Torremolinos** have good restaurants.

Málaga's wines

Málaga may seem an un-
likely place to make world-
class wine, with its near
desert-like climate and its
precipitous hills overlooking the gleaming Mediter-
ranean. The truth is that
Málaga is one of Spain's
most historic DOs. With
3000 hours of uninterrupt-
ed sun, very low rain, an av-
erage temperature of 18.5°C
(65°F) annually, and just an
occasional hard frost well
inland in winter, you've got
near perfect sweet win-
emaking conditions. Má-
laga wines once conquered
important overseas markets
much as sherry did. While
sherry sold to the British
Empire, Málaga found
eager customers in Imperial
Russia and German-speak-
ing countries.

Two World Wars and the
Russian Revolution played
havoc with Málaga's best
markets, as did the phyl-
loxera infestation. Málaga
once counted on 160,000
hectares (395,000 acres) of
vineyards. Today the DO
has 1,030 hectares (2,545
acres).

Still, Málaga is undergo-
ing an exciting renaissance,
with great wines being
made. Some producers

are tiny, such as **Bodega
Antigua Casa de Guardia**,
which produces around
4,000 bottles from 10
hectares (25 acres). Others,
such as **Bodegas Málaga
Virgen**, are much bigger
concerns.

Málaga wines are made
principally from two grape
varieties: Moscatel and
Pedro Ximénez. What
this means, basically, is
that there are three main
types of wines you can buy:
Moscatel-based wines; Pe-
dro Ximénez; and blends.

Bodegas

When Scholtz Hermanos
closed its doors for the
last time, the Málaga wine
industry lost a jewel in its
crown. Still, look out for
any old bottles of Scholtz
Hermanos you can find, as
they are well worth tasting.
Two wines you simply
have to try, although it will
almost certainly be impossible to track down their
original cellars because
these are small and not
always manned, include:
Molino Real Mountain
Wine, Cía. De Vinos Telmo
Rodríguez; and Jorge Or-
doñez Old Vines Muscat,
Bodegas Jorge Ordóñez &
Co, Almachar, Málaga.

BODEGAS & MORE

Bodegas Málaga Virgen
SA Autovía A-92, Km 132
29520 Fuente de Piedra
Tel: 952 319 454
bodegas@bodegasmalagavirgen.com
www.bodegasmalagavirgen.com

Málaga styles

Málaga wine comes in styles ranging from *Málaga Seco*, a full-bodied apéritif, to the more traditional sweet dessert wines. At their best these are unctuously smooth wines, with a raisiny aroma and flavor, and an intensity that lingers in the mouth.

Some Málaga styles go back in history to Shakespearean times. Alcohol varies, but is usually 15 to 18 percent.

Seco Amber in color, full-bodied but fermented to dryness.

Lágrima Made from the free-run juice of the grapes; dark, intense and sweet.

Pedro Ximénez (PX) Made from grape of that name, usually darker than Moscatel; sweet.

Moscatel Usually golden in color. Ranging from very sweet to relatively dry.

Solera Smooth, often dark in color.

Trasañejo Very old and rare, may have been aged for over 30 years. A treat.

Guinda A rare, ancient style.

Mountain The name used for Málaga in Shakespeare's time.

From Málaga to Jerez

From Málaga you have a choice of routes to the "Sherry Triangle." The first follows the coast along the AP-7 to Algeciras, then the A-381. The second is a more complicated inland route.

The Costas

The N-340 takes you along the length of the Costa del Sol and then continues to the quieter Costa de la Luz before reaching sherry country. The Costa del Sol is one of Spain's premier tourist destinations, an

Bodegas of Gonzalez Byass,
Jerez de la Frontera

(FERNANDO MADARIAGA/ICEX)

almost unbroken chain of beach resorts. The Costa de la Luz remains largely unspoiled and undiscovered.

Pueblos Blancos

An alternative route leads through the wild and rugged Serranía de Ronda and passes some picturesque *Pueblos Blancos* or "white villages," their houses white-washed, their roofs a colorful jumble of terracotta tiles. Leave Málaga on the A-397 and head for the hilltop town of Ronda.

Ronda

Ronda is a wonderful town. It is divided by a dramatic gorge bridged by the impressive **Puente Nuevo**. Its old quarter has an interesting Collegiate church, the **Palacio del Marqués de Salvatierra**, and the oldest bullring in Spain. The steep cliffs offer breathtaking views over the countryside.

Ronda was the scene of a mass execution during the Civil War. Hundreds of Nationalists were forced over the edge of the perilous gorge to their deaths, an episode which Hemingway describes in his novel *For Whom the Bell Tolls*.

Arcos de la Frontera

From Ronda the A-376 and then A-374 continue past the pretty town of Grazalema and the National Park of El Bosque to the town of Arcos de la Frontera. Set

on a high hill overlooking the Guadalete, the town has some spectacular views. Its Parador on the central square is an excellent place to stay the night. From Arcos the A-382 leads directly to Jerez.

Sherry
Sherry Country

The province of Cádiz containing what is known as the "Sherry Triangle" is famous throughout Spain. For centuries it has been celebrated for its *toros de lidia* (fighting bulls) bred on great ranches, its horses and the passionate nature of its people. Its fiestas, at which many of Spain's best flamenco dancers and bullfighters gather, are legendary.

(HAROLD HECKLE)

Sherry butts, Jerez de la Frontera

Cádiz itself, set on a promontory reaching into the sea, has a splendid historic past, being once the equivalent of Cape Canaveral as explorers set sail for the unknown lands of the New World. It was also from Cádiz that Spain's last mighty armada sailed, combined with Napoleon's French fleet, to meet Horatio Nelson at the battle of Trafalgar, the last great naval confrontation of the age of sail.

The sherry district, the Triangle, lies between the towns of Sanlúcar de Barrameda to the north on the Guadalquivir River; Jerez de la Frontera further south and east; and Puerto de Santa Maria on the coast, further south again.

Sherry Styles

Fino Pale and bone dry. The lightest of the sherry styles, it varies according to where it is aged. Those from Jerez are usually heavier in body and alcohol than those from Puerto.

Manzanilla Made only in Sanlúcar de Barrameda on the coast, Manzanillas develop a distinctive salty taste and are the driest and most delicate sherries of all. Their alcohol content is 15.5 to 17 percent.

Amontillado Amber in color, with more body than a Fino, Amontillados are dry, but the more commercial brands may be sweetened slightly. As with the darker Olorosos, these wines gather in intensity and complexity with age and have a distinctive nutty flavor. The alcohol content is 16 to 18 percent.

Oloroso Dark gold in color, very aromatic as the name implies (*olor* means aroma, *oloroso* means pungent), full-bodied and dry. Some commercial brands may also be sweetened slightly. The alcohol content is 18 to 20 percent.

Palo Cortado Perhaps the rarest style, it is described by the number of *rayas* or marks on the butt. You can have one, two or three *rayas*. Sometimes a blend of Palomino and Pedro Ximénez grapes, it can be like a cross between an

Oloroso and an Amontillado, full-bodied but slightly paler in color, and is well worth looking out for. As with Oloroso, the alcohol content is 18 to 20 percent.

Cream This is a very British invention, an Oloroso sweetened with Pedro Ximénez wine. Dark, almost mahogany in color, very smooth and richly sweet. A recent variation is the **Pale Cream**, which is a blend of Pedro Ximénez and Fino to produce a sweet but pale wine. The alcohol content in both is about 18 to 20 percent.

The Consejo Regulador de las Denominaciones de Origen de Jerez-Xérès-Manzanilla-Sanlúcar de Barrameda y Vinagre de Jerez

There are 64 *Bodegas de Crianza y Expedición* or sherry producers and shippers located within the Sherry Triangle. This denominated area covers 8,189 hectares (about 20,000 acres) and embraces about 3,700 individual vineyards of varying sizes. The best wines come from the parishes of Aniña, Balbaina and Los Tercios (for Finos); Macharnudo (for Amontillados); Carrascal (for Olorosos); and Miraflores and Torrebreba (for Manzanillas). The best soil is the chalky white *albariza*. Then come the *barros* with about 30 percent limestone and the *arenas*, sand with about 10 percent limestone.

The Palomino grape dominates the region and covers about 95 percent of the vineyard area. Smaller quantities of Pedro Ximénez and Moscatel are also grown for sweet wine production, though PX can be imported from Montilla-Moriles and Málaga. PX grapes are dried on esparto grass mats or more modern synthetic material to concentrate their sugar and produce super-sweet wines that are often used for blending in the production of sweet Amontillados, Creams and Pale Creams. Aged PX wines can be absolutely heavenly and have become very fashionable in recent years.

The website of the
Consejo Regulador—
www.sherry.org—is very
useful, containing as it does
up-to-date information on
every aspect of the region of
Jerez, including the fantastic vinegars made there. It
should be your first port of
call and constant reference
point when planning a visit
to Sherry Country.

Sherry and its traditions

Stemware

Catavinos (traditionally
called *Copitas* by the wine
trade) are the slim and elegant glasses in which sherry
is traditionally served in
Spain. They narrow at
the mouth to concentrate
aromas.

Principal grape varieties

The Palomino Fino grape
thrives in this warm, consistent climate, particularly
on chalky white *albariza* soil
and, before fortification,
produces pleasant but unremarkable wine. It is sherry's
aging and blending process

that makes it unique. PX is
grown in small quantities.

Aging the wine

Sherry is Spain's only truly
unique wine, produced and
aged in the Sherry Trian-
gle formed by the towns
of Jerez, Puerto de Santa
Maria and Sanlúcar de Barrameda. The solera system
concentrates the aromas
and flavors provided by a
happy combination of cli-
mate, soil and grape variety.
Sherry butts are piled up
to three layers high. The
ground level is referred
to as the *solera* (soil), from
where around a third of the
barrel is emptied for bottling. This is then topped
up from the barrels above
and fresh wine is added at
the top layer. The resulting process blends and ages
wine all at once.

Flor

After fermentation, the
wine is transferred to oak
butts that are loosely stop-
pered and never completely
filled. Flor (Spanish for
flower) begins to develop
on the wine's surface. Flor is
a layer of yeasts that forms
on the surface of the wine
and prevents oxidization by

(PHILIP CLARKE)

The Alcázar of Jerez de la Frontera, once a fortified palace belonging to the Muslim rulers of the region

insulating it. Over a period of six months it dies slowly, leaving the wine clear and ready for classification, depending on the thickness of the original flor.

Another of the peculiarities of sherry is that no two butts of wine develop in exactly the same manner. The task of the cellar master, or *capataz*, is to determine the style into which the wine will develop.

Usually the more delicate wines with the thickest flor will be classified as Finos or Amontillados, while those with the thinnest will become Olorosos. In a Palo Cortado the flor has often collapsed part of the way through the process. The level of collapse is measured on the outside of the barrel with one or more chalk marks, or *rayas*. Once classified, the wines are fortified and then introduced to the solera.

The solera system

The system's purpose is to produce wines of uniform quality and character. It involves several butts known as the *soleras* (bottom rows) and *criaderas* (the upper levels), usually placed one on top of the other. Wine is drawn from the *solera* level for further blending and bottling. More wine is then brought down to replace what was taken for bot-

tling from the first *criadera*, which is filled from the second *criadera* level, and so on. Continuity in style and character is ensured. The system has been copied all over the world, yet Spanish sherry remains unique in its subtle aromas and potent flavors—a great contribution to wine culture.

Jerez brandy

"*Jerezanos* created art with their wine, then made money with their brandy," goes a popular saying.

(CHRISTINE CLARK)

A cask of rare, very old Matusalem Oloroso sherry signed by Winston Churchill, at Gonzalez Byass, Jerez de la Frontera

Brandy de Jerez, whose production is controlled by its own Consejo Regulador, is different from the brandies made in most other parts of the world due to the use of the solera system. Jerez producers buy wine in other regions, mainly La Mancha, and often distil it there before transporting it to the sherry towns for aging and blending.

Most brandy is aged by a static process in a single cask or barrel. In Jerez, however, it goes through the solera system in a similar way to sherry, a process known as dynamic aging. The transfer of brandy from butt to butt ensures that it ages faster and more smoothly, while the addition of caramel, used in varying amounts by different houses, gives it smoky pungency, sweetness, color and depth of flavor. Some brandies are completely dry. At the popular end of the scale brandy can be fiery and harsh, used mainly as a cheap mixer and added to coffee to make the heart-starting *carajillo*. Premium brandy offers a fascinating range, from comparatively light dry to thicker, darker and sweeter *gran reservas*.

DO *Brandy de Jerez*

The DO Brandy de Jerez was established in 1988. It was the third brandy to be given its own denomination after Cognac and Armagnac. Strict regulations govern its aging:

Solera Aged for a minimum of six months in butt.

Reserva Aged for a minimum of one year in butt.

Gran Reserva Aged for a minimum of three years in butt. In practice, aging periods tend to be longer, with Gran Reservas often aged for six years or more.

Jerez de la Frontera

The largest of the three towns that make up the Sherry Triangle is more city than town, with several fine churches and historic buildings. Its 16th-century Collegiate Church (near González Byass and Domecq wineries) is set at the top of a wide flight of steps and is very attractive. Jerez also has a Moorish fortress, or **Alcázar**, dating back to the 12th century, and is the home of the Andalusian School of Equestrian Art, which regularly holds public displays of superb horsemanship.

The center of Jerez has the hallmarks of a prosperous city: office blocks, banks and restaurants packed at lunchtime with smartly dressed executives. Less impressive architecture, including unattractive suburbs and tall apartment blocks, have also encroached on the town. On the surface, Jerez is a normal, busy city in southern Spain. Just below the surface there lies magic.

Historic legacies

The exact date of Jerez's foundation is unknown, but it stands in a corner of Andalusia that has benefited from a succession of foreign influences, many of which have left their mark on its towns and the character of its people. Even before the Moorish occupation in AD 711, the area had witnessed the arrival and departure of Phoenicians, Greeks, Carthaginians, Romans, Vandals and Visigoths. The Moors stayed for seven and a half centuries and their influence, as elsewhere in Andalusia, can be clearly seen. More recently, the British established visible roots, too.

The British connection

British merchants began to trade in the region in the early 14th century, and commerce has flourished just about ever since. They established companies like Sandeman, Duff Gordon, Osborne, Williams & Humbert, Croft, John Harvey and many more. Some were wholly British-owned, others were the fruit of successful partnerships with local families. One, González Byass, has reverted from a world-famous partnership to being wholly Spanish. These companies adapted the product to the tastes of their clients, adding sweetening wine to make up different, supposedly smooth, styles such as Milk and Cream.

Great Britain became, and continues to be, the largest and most consistent market for sherry in the world, bigger even than Spain. The British connection brought along vestiges of British imperial culture such as the **Polo Club of Jerez**, which remains extremely popular. It was

(FERNANDO MADAR #GA/ LCE)

An old sherry solera at Álvaro Domecq, Jerez de la Frontera

founded in 1874, a mere four years after the sport was introduced to England from India (Jerez also attracted army officers who were stopping off at Gibraltar on their way to or from India), and even today it is surprising how many Jerezanos have British names and speak English with an impeccable accent.

The vaults of Jerez

Behind high, whitewashed walls and wrought-iron gates you'll find another, almost secret world. Here historic long, cool bodegas with high vaulted ceilings and swept earth floors are crammed with rows of dark oak butts full of pungent, maturing sherry. Colorful, immaculately-kept gardens

Montilla

shaded by trees lead on to inner patios with flickering fountains. This is a hidden city that one cannot help falling in love with.

Bodegas of Jerez

Most of Jerez's leading bodegas welcome visitors and have conducted tours of their premises, which invariably end up with a good-humored tasting. The most popular are the city's two giants, **González Byass** and **Pedro Domecq**, two firms that personify the sherry industry. Both establishments are almost small towns in their own right, with tree-lined streets separating their numerous bodegas. In González Byass, the most notable of these are the Gran Bodega Tio Pepe and the circular La Concha, designed by Gustav Eiffel, the 19th-century engineer. Domecq has El Molino with a collection of ancient barrels signed by such historic figures as the Duke of Wellington, as well as the Mezquita, built along the lines of the famous mosque in Córdoba.

Visits to these companies are efficiently conducted but they have the disadvantage that you are often shown around in large groups. Many travellers may prefer to visit the smaller

(HAROLD HECKLE)

firms. Visits can be arranged online without difficulty once you find your feet in the city. The Consejo Regulador's site, www.sherry.org, contains contact details for all bodegas.

Smaller bodegas

Try the relatively unknown but very charming **Rey Fernando de Castilla** which produces a wonderful range of high quality sherries and brandies. The elegant and very English **Williams & Humbert** bodega (with wine museum) was founded in 1877 and, if you can get access, is probably the most charming of them all.

El Puerto de Santa María

Lying on the coast 10 km (6 miles) from Jerez is Puerto de Santa María. In the past most sherry used to be shipped from the small docks here, before Cádiz replaced it in the early part of the last century. From the bridge at the mouth of its river there is a fabulous view over the bay to the distant port of Cádiz.

Puerto is much smaller than Jerez, but it is a lively town with first-class seaside restaurants. An enjoyable evening can be spent just doing the rounds of its excellent tapas bars near the center, which buzz with life at the weekends. There are good beaches on the Atlantic, notably at **Valde-lagrana**, and, for yachting enthusiasts, the modern Puerto Sherry marina. On its outskirts there is also the best hotel in the area, the **Caballo Blanco**.

Puerto's bodegas

Since it is on the coast, Puerto has a different climate from Jerez. It is cooled by the sea and consequently has a higher level of humidity. As a result, its dry sherries are also slightly different, being lower in alcohol and, some would say, having greater finesse and a more generous aroma of flor.

Puerto is also a great brandy center, the home of **Osborne** and **Fernando A. de Terry**. These are two of the leading brands in Spain, the latter being famous for its white Cartujano horses. It is these that led, through selective breeding and training in Vienna since 1580, to the Lipizzaners used at the Spanish Riding School there. A third large concern based in the town is the family-run firm of Luis Caballero.

It is Osborne and its affiliate Duff Gordon that dominate the town. **El Tiro**, Osborne's great brandy bodega, is on the left as you enter Puerto. In the center of the town is another major complex, which houses its *soleras* and is open to the public. The older wines here are staggeringly good in quality.

Sanlúcar de Barrameda

Sanlúcar, the third sherry town, is at the mouth of the Guadalquivir River, looking across at **Coto de Doñana**, one of the largest and most fragile nature reserves in Europe. It is some 20 km (12 miles) from Jerez along a small road that leads through the heart of the region's *albariza* country, and it was from this small port that Columbus sailed on his first great voyage of discovery, a cause of major celebrations here.

Sanlúcar may not be as beautiful as Cádiz, but it has good, modestly priced hotels and its central square is abuzz with lively bars. Try the **Marisquería Juan Carlos** for good cuisine or **La Gitana** for tapas. Excellent fish restaurants along the river offer a relaxed atmosphere. Sitting al fresco for a meal of recently landed, lightly grilled fish with a bottle of chilled Manzanilla is one of the great pleasures of a visit to Spain. Also try the local *langostinos* (tiger prawns).

A visit to the Doñana park, with its 250 species of wildlife, is also a must, as are visits to the palaces of the Dukes of Medina Sidonia (one of whom led the ill-fated "Invincible Armada" against England in 1588) and of the Montpensiers, as well as to the home of the Marqués de Casa Arizón, a leading Indies trader.

Manzanilla

It's difficult to pinpoint why this wine is so distinctive. Some believe its delicious, salty tang is the result of its aging by the sea, a theory supported by the fact that if a butt is taken back to Jerez it slowly takes on the character of a typical Fino. Whatever the reason, Manzanilla is the driest and I would say the most delicate of all sherries. Look out for the rare Manzanilla Pasada,

a wine that has been aged for longer, giving it greater color and body, and the delicious Manzanilla *en rama*.

Sanlúcar's bodegas

Sanlúcar is dominated by **Antonio Barbadillo**, a company that accounts for some 70 percent of the world's Manzanilla production. Barbadillo also has fantastic supplies of ancient, rare wines. The firm dates back to 1821. Its sprawling complex of bodegas, based around a beautiful old Andalusian mansion, occupies most of the upper part of the town. Closer to the center is the much smaller **Vinícola Hidalgo**, a family company whose charming and picturesque winery is well worth a visit.

BODEGAS & MORE

JEREZ
(Please refer to website: www.sherry.org)
Domecq
Cuesta Espíritu Santo s/n
Tel: 952 247 236
sebastianmendezgomez@
pernod-ricard-espana.com

González Byass
Calle Manuel María
González 12
11403 Jerez de la Frontera
Tel: 956 357 000
reservas@gonzalezbyass.es
www.bodegastiopepe.com

Harveys
Calle Pintor
Muñoz Cebrián s/n
11401 Jerez de la Frontera
Tel: 956 151 500
visitas@bodegasharveys.com
www.bodegasharveys.com

Emilio Lustau SA
Calle Arcos, 53
11402 Jerez de la Frontera
Tel: 956 341 597
jw@lustau.es
www.emilio-lustau.com

Williams & Humbert Ltd
Ctra Nacional IV - Km 641
11408 Jerez de la Frontera
Tel: 956 353 406
visitas@williams-humbert.com
www.williams-humbert.com

Rey Fernando de Castilla
Calle Jardinillo 7-11, 11404
Jerez de la Frontera
Tel: 956 182 454
bodegas@fernandodecastilla.com
www.fernandodecastilla.com

PUERTO DE
SANTA MARIA
Bodegas Osborne
Los Moros 7
11500 El Puerto
de Santa Maria
Tel: 956 869 100
Visitas.bodegas@osborne.es
www.osborne.es

(HAROLD HECKLE)

A typical sherry glass (called a *catavinos*), reflected in a pool of water atop a barrel

SANLUCAR DE
BARRAMEDA

SANLUCAR DE
BARRAMEDA
Antonio Barbadillo SA
Luis de Eguilaz, 11
11540 Sanlucar de Barrameda
Tel: 956 385 500
barbadillo@barbadillo.com
www.barbadillo.com

Vinícola Hidalgo y Cia SA
Banda de la Playa, 42
11540 Sanlucar de Barrameda
Tel: 956 385 304
bodegashidalgo@lagitana.es
www.lagitana.es

Food and festivals of Andalusia

Andalusian food

In recent years Andalucian food has become very refined and today matches the great quality of the best wines of the region.

Ham, fish and vegetables

With coasts on the Mediterranean and the Atlantic, the fish—ranging from whitebait and sardines to shrimp and lobster—is excellent. It can be enjoyed closest to the sea in the beach restaurants of Málaga and Sanlúcar. Andalusia is also the producer of some very good cured ham, *jamón serrano*. The Jabugo region, in the province of Huelva, and Trevélez in the Sierra Nevada produce excellent examples. Its top quality olive oil, almonds and sherry vinegar are world class. Vegetables, the basis of the famous gazpacho (chilled soup), are increasing in quality and quantity as a result of the great agricultural developments in Almería and the Guadalquivir valley, which has converted this part of Spain into the California of Europe.

Tapas

Among the most charming aspect of Andalusian cuisine are the tapas, the small dishes or appetizers served with drinks, which can vary from simple plates of olives, peanuts or almonds to more elaborate offerings such as fried squid, shrimp, slices of ham or tortilla (Spanish omelet), Russian-style potato salad, or *pinchos*, cubes of spiced meat grilled on skewers.

The perfect accompaniment to a glass of chilled Fino or dry Montilla, tapas are served in most bars of the south of Spain but are the specialty of Seville and Almería, where several of these dishes often make up a meal. Try *riñones al jerez* (kidneys in a sherry sauce).

Festivals

Andalusia is a land of fiestas. Córdoba has its Courtyard Fair in May, Granada its Corpus Christi and the International Festival of Music and Dance (June and July). Seville has the world famous Holy Week, and its **Feria de Abril**, which is a frenzy of music, dancing and horse parades. All are unforgettable.

Jerez has two annual fairs that celebrate the three things that its people love best: wine, horses, and flamenco dancing and music. The first, the **Feria del Caballo**, is in early to mid May with horse racing, parades and horseback bullfighting. The horses and riders of the Real Escuela are housed in an immaculate 19th century palace, el Palacio Recreo de las Cadenas, and such is the majesty of the spectacle the first sight of them is enough to take your

breath away. Try and see the show: *Cómo Bailan los Caballos Andaluces*.

The second is the **Feria de la Vendimia** in September, when girls carry the first grapes to be crushed and blessed at the Collegiate Church, doves are released to the sound of ringing bells and a party of drinking and dancing begins.

QUICK TIPS
If you are short on time, try these bodegas (all located in Jerez):

Gonzalez Byass
Large and stately, this bodega is tailor-made to suit sherry lovers in search of the best; a complete compendium of styles awaits the visitor. Try VORS wines.

Domecq
History and nobility combine as you walk under gates etched with the date 1730. An impressive range to taste. Try VORS wines.

Lustau
A new angle in an ancient winemaking land. Clearly focused styles aimed at today's consumer. Smaller and more personal than the big league. Try VOS wines.

TOP 10 WINES TO TRY DURING A FERIA

Barbadillo Manzanilla en Rama

For a light, slightly salty and tangy aperitif at lunchtime nothing beats the natural, un-fussed quality of an *en rama* Manzanilla, and Barbadillo make some of the best.

Gonzalez Byass Tio Pepe Fino

To accompany the first tapas of the day, Tio Pepe encompasses the very essence of Fino as we have come to understand it today. Perfect with *boquerones* (small, fresh anchovies).

Osborne Fino Quinta

For a true understanding of what a Fino means to a Spaniard, you simply have to accompany a fish soup or gazpacho with the wonderfully mature quality of Fino Quinta.

Gonzalez Byass Amontillado del Duque

Sherry experts have always known that the real fun begins with Amontillado. For an insight into what it's all about try this with lobster.

Osborne AOS Solera

The mellow, well-rested and matured character of this superb Amontillado will only reinforce your conviction that sherry is beyond price.

Domecq Amontillado 51-1a

When you want to fortify yourself for the afternoon's

Osborne, Jerez de la Frontera

(FERNANDO MADARIAGA/ICEX)

A sherry barrel showing how flor floats to stop oxidation

(PHILIP CLARK)

activities, nothing will bring you back to life after the siesta like the glorious power of this eternal wine.

**Gonzalez Byass
Matusalem Oloroso**
As the evening wears on, Olorosos come into their own, but few can match the brilliance of Matusalem.

**Osborne
PΔP Palo Cortado**
A hint of sweetness just lifts the palate and the wonderful aromas linger with you for ages. Gorgeous.

**Sanchez Romate
La Sacristia PX**
Dark and beautiful, deep and rich on the nose, this PX is sheer heaven to finish off the evening meal.

Osborne PX Viejo
Just to remind you why sherry is unique, this is one to take home with you, the embodiment of classic sweet wine.

WHERE TO STAY AND EAT

Córdoba

El Caballo Rojo
Cardenal Herrero, 28
14003 Córdoba
Tel: 957 475 375
www.elcaballorojo.com
One of the pioneers of
Moorish-Jewish fusion
cuisine in Spain.

Restaurante El Churrasco
Calle Romero, 16
14003 Córdoba
Tel: 957 290 819
www.elchurrasco.com
Good meat and fish in the
heart of the Judería. Ask to
see the wine cellar!

Restaurante Almudaina
Plaza Campo Santo
De Los Mártires, 1
14004 Córdoba
Tel: 957 474 342
Palatial setting with a patio.

**Taberna Casa Pepe
"De la Judería"**
Calle Romero, 1
14003 Córdoba
Tel: 957 200 744/
     957 200 766
casapepe@casapepedelajuderia.com

Casa Miguel
Plaza San Miguel, 7
Córdoba
Tel: 957 478 328

Casa Rubio
Puerta De Almodóvar, 3
14003 Córdoba
Tel: 957 420 853

Jerez

Tendido-6
Calle Circo, 10
11405 Jerez de la Frontera
Tel: 956 330 374
info@tendido6.com
www.tendido6.com
Opposite the Bullring. (R)

La Mesa Redonda
Manuel de la Quintana, 3
11402 Jerez de la Frontera
Tel: 956 340 069 (R)

Gaitán
Calle Gaitán, 3
11403 Jerez de la Frontera
Tel: 956 345 859 (R)

Málaga

Café de París
Vélez Málaga, 8
29016 Málaga
Tel: 952 225 043
Elegant and sophisticated
(R)

Casa Pedro
Playa de El Palo, Cra
Almería, Málaga
Tel: 952 229 0003
Specialty: Fish (R)

Montilla

Hotel Don Gonzalo
Ctra Córdoba-Málaga
Km 47, 14450 Montilla
Tel: 957 650 658

Las Camachas
Avda de Europa 3
14550 Montilla
Tel: 957 650 004 (R)

For a full list of where to stay and eat, please consult the Montilla website:
www.montilla.es

El Puerto de Santa María

Los Portales
Calle Ribera del Marisco
7, 11500 El Puerto de Santa María
Tel: 956 542 116
restaurante@losportales.com
restaurantelosportales.com (R)

La Goleta
Carretera Fuentebravía
Km 0.7
El Puerto de Santa María
Tel: 956 854 232 (R)

Las Boveda
Virgen de los Milagros, 2
El Puerto de Santa María
Tel: 956 540 440 (R)

Ronda

Pedro Romero
Virgen de la Paz, 18
29400 Ronda
Tel: 952 871 110
pedroromero@ronda.net
In front of the bullring. (R)

Parador Nacional
Plaza de España
29400 Ronda
Tel: 952 877 500
The restaurant offers
breathtaking views. (H)

Sanlúcar de Barrameda

The restaurants on the
beach can't be recommend-
ed too highly, try several
before leaving. The following are outstanding:

Bigote
Avenida Bajo De Guía, 10
11540 Sanlúcar de
Barrameda
Tel: 956 362 696
www.restaurantecasabigote.com

Casa Juan
Avenida Bajo De Guía, 26
11540 Sanlúcar de
Barrameda
Tel: 956 362 695 (R)

Restaurante Mirador
Doñana
Bajo de Guia s/n, 11540
Sanlúcar de
Barrameda
Tel: 956 364 205
info@miradordonana.com
www.miradordonana.com (R)

Los Helechos
Plaza de Madre de Dios, 9
11540 Sanlúcar de
Barrameda
Tel: 956 361 349
www.hotelloshelechos.com
(H)

A view of the Alcázar gardens, Seville, the capital of Andalusia, with the Giralda bell tower in the center.

(PHILIP CLARK)

NORTHWEST SPAIN

O VER THE PAST COUPLE OF DECADES North-west Spain has become a thriving center for high-quality wine thanks to brave and ambitious programs to rebuild its vineyards in the wake of phylloxera and its effects. Initially, government authorities had opted for high yields, but by the mid 1970s it was clear that quality not quantity was the most likely path to job security and employment creation. High-cropping varieties such as the white Palomino (famous for sherry) and Garnacha Tintorera were largely grubbed up to be replaced by local varieties that had been recovered from the brink of extinction. Among the vines saved from oblivion were Albariño, Godello and Mencía.

Galicia

For Galicia, life changed forever when Columbus sailed to America. From being *Finis Terre*, literally the ends of the earth, this green and pleasant land went on to become yet another beautiful and slightly inaccessible seafood-lover's paradise. Exposed as it is at Europe's western tip, Galicia is more weather-beaten and rain-swept than any other part of Spain. Despite its relative isolation, it has been a tourist destination for centuries, attracting pilgrims to the relics of St James. Modern roads and airports have made Galicia much more accessible, though it still retains some of the magic and mystery of its erstwhile remoteness. Just as in the Middle Ages, no tour of Spain can be complete without a visit to **Santiago de Compostela**, in whose splendid cathedral lay the sacred remains. For a wine pilgrim the regions of Rías Baixas, and increasingly Ribeira Sacra and

《 Detail of one of the spires of the Cathedral of Santiago de Compostela, Galicia

NORTHWEST SPAIN

Ribeiro, act as magnets.

Even without its wine Galicia would be worth a visit as it is one of the most beautiful corners of Spain. A land of fjord-like sea inlets (known as *rías*) and steep green valleys with fast-running streams, Galicia is blessed with a wealth of evocative misty landscapes that cause its inhabitants to suffer from deep homesickness (*morriña*) when away for too long. Food and wine are also sources of great pride for Galicians (*Gallegos*). Modern technology has revealed its native and once-rare grape varieties to be genuine stars, a perfect accompaniment to superb local shellfish and seafood, which you simply have to try. Beware, Galicia's climate is milder than you might expect and also much wetter. If you are after luminous skies then try to go during the summer months, and take a raincoat.

Galicia has much to recommend it. Where once there were lovely if slightly rustic and unreliable wines, today there are five regions that are worthy of serious exploration, denominated and regulated by official bodies. Three, Rías Baixas, Ribeira Sacra and Ribeiro, ought to feature in any initial trip to the area with the others providing an excellent excuse to return.

Rías Baixas

If ever there was a reason needed to prompt a visit to Galicia then it has to be the DO Rías Baixas. From Santiago head south on the N-550 or the AP-9 (toll) until you reach the town of Caldas de Reis. Take the N-640 to Vilagarcia and follow the PO-549 along the gorgeous coast to the port of Cambados, around which the vineyards of Salnés are situated.

If you continue south along the coast on the PO-549, then PO-550, you'll reach Pontevedra. The N-550 and AP-9 will then take you further south to Tui on the Portuguese border. From Tui once again take the PO-550 west to explore the sub-region of O Rosal. Backtrack eastward to Salvaterra de Miño and you hit the sub-region of Condado de Tea (teh-ah).

Ribeiro

Ribeiro, once famous more for the shape of its wine

The Rías Baixas, seen through a glass of Albariño

(HAROLD HECKLE)

goblets than the contents, is very much worth a visit. Inland or east along the Miño river on the A-52 you'll see Ribadavia, the capital of Ribeiro. Ribeiro wine is one of Spain's recent hits.

Ribeira Sacra

On the eastern edge of Galicia you'll find the steep-sided V-shaped valleys, not dissimilar to those in Porto, with ancient, carefully crafted terraces, where some of Spain's most interesting white wines are being made.

Valdeorras

On Galicia's eastern border, Valdeorras is home to some fabulous Godello whites and Mencía reds, not to mention delicious red peppers.

The wines of Galicia

Modern technology has virtually reinvented the wine map. Twenty years ago only a handful of local Galicians had any idea of the potential waiting to be unleashed. Many will tell you that they always knew about these wines and that their recent discovery has only made them sought-after and expensive. The truth is that old-timers would barely recognize the modern, subtle and delicate wines made today. A traveller can still share in the excitement of reveling in something relatively new.

Native grape varieties

The great secret of Galicia, as with any remarkable region, is the fantastic combination of local grape varieties with soil and weather conditions.

Spain's fame has traditionally lain with decent red wines and sherries, bigger mouthfuls than most people are prepared to combine with delicate seafood. In came beautifully fermented Albariño, Loureiro, Treixadura and most recently Godello. Modern clonal research and the introduction of cultivation studies as well as vinification techniques have heralded unparalleled levels of quality and sophistication undreamed of not long ago, whatever the locals might tell you.

The new age

Phylloxera hit northwest Spain very hard, devastating wine production that had dated from Roman times. In order to recover quickly from the catastrophe, vineyards were restocked with high-yielding varieties like Palomino and Garnacha Tintorera (notoriously difficult to make classy wines from). While these grapes were heavy croppers, the wines they made were really the standard fare of cooperatives and bulk wine establishments.

Then in the mid 1980s agricultural experts began investigating varieties that almost became extinct in the phylloxera disaster. Their aim was to see if quality winemaking could be fomented in the area. Among their discoveries were the grapes mentioned above, including Mencía

The Atlantic off A Guarda, Pontevedra, Galicia

and some varieties yet to make it to commercial bottling.

The first region to make a breakthrough on domestic and then world markets was Rías Baixas, which came on stream in 1988. Almost overnight traditional, older-style Ribeiro and Valdeorras wines were outshone by its new-age *blancos*. Ribeira Sacra, Bierzo and Ribeiro have followed suit. Thanks to careful research that has included investigating which soil and solar orientation best suits each grape, the northwest of Spain has established a well-earned reputation for

(FERNANDO BRIONES/ICEX)

producing the country's best white wines.

Rías Baixas

Rías Baixas is divided into five sub-zones: Val do Salnés around the mouth of the Umia River; Condado de Tea on the right bank of the Miño River; O Rosal on the northern bank of the Miño near the Atlantic; Soutomaior at the mouth of the Verdugo River and Ribera do Ulla on both banks of the Ulla River.

In Salnés, wine is made entirely from Albariño, but other varieties are used in Rosal and Condado, principally Loureira in the first and Treixadura in the second. These as well as varieties like Caiño make up only a small percentage of the total blend. The quality of Rías Baixas' wines is based primarily on the subtle and vibrant character of Albariño.

Albariño

Legend has it that Albariño is descended from Riesling (some will mention Chardonnay, too) brought to these parts by German (or French) monks on a pilgrimage to Santiago. The theory may be fanciful, but the three varieties do share some characteristics.

Albariño is a thin-skinned terpenic grape (terpenes are a class of flavor compound also found in Muscat and Gewürztraminer) traditionally planted *en parra* or on granite stone pergolas. This gives it maximum exposure to air and sun. The technique is aimed at lowering the incidence of fungal disease. The wines tend to be relatively low in alcohol and high in fresh acidity, making them crisp, delicate, complex and often subtly honeyed.

Albariño is usually drunk young, but bodegas are finding their wines can age successfully and even improve in their second year. Barrique-fermented Albariños or those with a few months of oak aging definitely need time in bottle, often drinking well in their third year. While wood gives them an extra dimension, it can also dull their raciness and mask delicate fruit. In southern sub-zones, Treixadura and Loureiro can be added to give aromatic character.

Albariño is an expensive grape to cultivate properly, so its wines are not cheap.

Ruta del Vino

Rías Baixas has an organized wine route, or *Ruta do Viño* in Galician. A fair number of bodegas take part in the scheme and their geographical position is indicated (often in a typically Spanish, slightly obscure fashion) by a signpost depicting a wine glass. Some of these have become as much a part of the landscape here as the famous *horreos*, raised pagoda-like corn stores, and *cruceiros*, crosses on the side of the road.

Ruta bodegas are open

most days except public holidays. Make sure you arm yourself with the very useful brochure (*Ruta del Vino de la DO Rías Baixas*), which you should be able to obtain at tourist information points and most bodegas. As well as providing maps giving the location of all these bodegas, the brochure is an invaluable guide to other places of interest along the route such as churches, castles and archeological sites.

Santiago de Compostela

Santiago is a great place to stay, starting with the fabulous **Parador de los Reyes Católicos** (possibly the most spectacular Parador in Spain). Good websites to consult are www.compostelavirtual.com and http://santiago-de-compostela.salir.com.

Santiago's natural center of gravity is its venerable **Cathedral of St. James**, a

(FERNANDO BRIONES/ICEX)

Viña Mein in Leiro, Galicia, producers of some of the best-selling Ribeiro wines

tourist magnet for centuries. Inside you'll still find an ancient incense burner called Botafumeiro (originally used to soften the impact of the smell of hundreds of weary pilgrims who had arrived after lengthy pilgrimages from as far away as Britain, Rome and Germany). It is still used during solemn occasions. It swings, spreading the aroma of incense the length of the majestic aisle, propelled by a handful of monks. Take a conducted tour of the cathedral, which includes stepping out on to the roof, on which pigs and chickens were once kept.

Life fans out from the cathedral square, once reputed to have been the field in which St. James's sarcophagus was found resting under star-studded skies (*campus stellae*, or the field of stars in Latin). Naturally, religion forms an important backdrop to Santiago, but soon you'll discover the warmth of the Gallego welcome and the bounty of their food and quite remarkable wines (especially the whites).

FOR FURTHER INFORMATION

The first thing to do is to visit the Rías Baixas website: www.doriasbaixas.com. This is the website of The Consejo Regulador Denominación de Origen "Rías Baixas,"
Palacio de Mugártegui,
Plaza de Pedreira 10
36002 Pontevedra
Tel: 986 854 850
consejo@doriasbaixas.com

(HAROLD HECKLE)

Steep terraces of vineyards on the banks of the Sil River in the DO Ribeira Sacra contain crushed slate soils

Albariño Country

Cambados

After the touristy bustle of Santiago, this is a quiet, charming fishing village with an impressive square, **Plaza de Fefiñanes**, and the ruins of the Santa Marina Dozo monastery. The Tourist Office is just off the main square in Rua Novedades. Cambados also has an excellent, centrally located Parador and makes an ideal overnight stop. Bodegas around Cambados are on small side roads so it's best to ask at each one for directions to the next or make sure you have SatNav.

The bodegas of Salnés

Cambados is at the heart of the Salnés sub-zone and a day can easily be spent visiting its bodegas. Within the city is the 17th-century Palacio de Fefiñanes in the main square. A short drive outside Cambados is **Vilariño** and the larger **Bodegas Vilariño-Cambados** located on a hill with views over the town. Not far is **Agro de Bazán**, a wine

estate of 11 hectares (27 acres) of vineyard near the town of Tremoedo, with a charismatic winery built in 1987 but following local architectural traditions.

For lunch either return to Cambados or drive down to the historic town of Vilanova de Arousa.

Near the town of Ribadumia you'll find the small, family-owned **Castro Martín**. Nearby is **Pazo de Barrantes**, owned by the Count of Creixell, also proprietor of Rioja's famous Marqués de Murrieta. Make sure you book your visit beforehand.

While here, visit the magical **Praia a Lanzada** beach before sunset. Along the way is the modern, impressive **Bodegas Salnesur** near the town of Castrelo. The coast road leads to Pontevedra, a city well worth visiting, not least because on the way, in Meaño, you'll find **Agnusdei**, a modern winery producing award-winning Albariño.

O Rosal

At Pontevedra get ready for a great day out by taking the N-550 south. You may want to stop at Arcade, a

Rías Baixas

(HAROLD HECKLE)

port just south of the city at the tip of the Ría de Vigo, famed for its oysters. Otherwise continue to the border town of Tui (with its interesting fortified church and a good Parador) and turn west on the C-550.

Not far inland you'll find O Rosal. **Lagar de Cervera**, a beautiful bodega owned by the same families as La Rioja Alta, produces great Albariño. You might want to try your hand at the local brandy, a transparent spirit called Orujo, somewhat like Grappa. Just south is Fornelos, where you should visit **Lagar de Fornelos** before visiting the windmills at Folón and then have lunch in A Guarda, a town famous for its fish restaurants. To walk it off go **Monte Santa Tecla** with its great views over the estuary of the Miño and the excavations of a Celtic village.

Condado

More glorious bodegas await you, this time in Condado. Drive back to Tui and then follow the river Miño east toward Salvaterra de Miño. Before you reach the town you'll see signs to **Granja Fillaboa**. This delightful winery is approached by a medieval hump-backed bridge and stands in its own vineyards, with a 19th-century stone building at its center. Ask how to get to the 16th-century **Pazo San Mauro**, a place of pilgrimage.

BODEGAS & MORE

CAMBADOS
Bodegas del Palacio de Fefiñanes
Plaza de Fefiñanes s/n
36630 Cambados
Tel: 986 542 204
fefinanes@fefinanes.com

www.fefinanes.com
Housed in a 17th-century
palace.

VILANOVA DE
AROUSA
Agro de Bazán Granbazán
Lugar de Tremoedo, 46
36628 Vilanova de Arousa
Tel: 986 555 562
agrodebazan@agrodebazan.es

RIBADUMIA
Bodegas Pazo de Barrantes
Finca Pazo de Barrantes
36636 Ribadumia
Tel: 986 718 211
www.pazodebarrantes.com

PONTEVEDRA
**Agnusdei Call Grupo
Vinum Terrae**
Lugar de Axis - Simes s/n
36968 Meaño
Tel: 986 747 566
comercial@vinumterrae.com

FORNELOS
Lagar de Cervera
Barrio Cruces, O Rosal
36778 Fornelos
Tel: 986 625 875
www.riojalta.com

SALVATERRA
DE MIÑO
Pazo San Mauro
Porto 36450
Salvatierra de Miño
Tel: 986 658 285
info@pazosanmauro.com

www.marquesdevargas.com
Owned by Rioja producer
Marqués de Vargas.

Bodegas Fillaboa
Lugar de Fillaboa
Salvaterra de Miño
36459 Pontevedra
Tel: 986 658 132
info@bodegasfillaboa.com
www.fillaboa.es
Booking essential.

Ribeira Sacra

One look at the beauti-
ful, ancient and extremely
steep-sided slate terraces of
Ribeira Sacra will convince
you instantly of the quality
potential here. Wines have
been made here since time
immemorial but its 3,000
hectares only received DO
status in 1996. There are five
fascinating sub-zones. Wines
can be made of Godello,
Albariño, Loureira, Treixe-
dura, Torrontés and Doña
Blanca but it is Godello that
is the indisputable star.

Pena das Donas (a *dona*
is a mythological figure, a
female elf, in Galician) is
located in the tiny hamlet of
Ribas del Sil west of Ourense
on the N-120. The winery
owns one hectare and oversees another two. Owner
Jesús Vázquez Rodríguez
cultivates vines on steep

V-sided hillsides. Try their Almalarga, 100 percent Godello.

Three rivers—the Miño, Sil and Bubal—drain Ribeira Sacra. The Roman port of Portus Polumbaris on the Sil was used to export prized wines from a local patch called Amandi. **Adega Algueira** in the curiously named town of Sober is where owner Fernando "Algueira" González works ten hectares that reflect the mineral quality of slate soils.

Dominio do Bibei in Langullo, Manzaneda, is 550 meters (1,800 ft) above sea level on hillsides surrounded by vineyards and mountain herbs. This winery is very hard to get into, but worth the effort. It is part owned by clothing magnate Javier Dominguez. He says Godello is "beyond doubt, Spain's greatest white grape." Try his amazing wines.

FOR FURTHER INFORMATION
DO Ribeira Sacra
Comercio 6-8
Monforte de Lemos
Tel: 982 410 968
info@ribeirasacra.org
www.ribeirasacra.org
The website and office have a section dedicated to tourism which is incredibly

(HAROLD HECKLE)

Young girls in traditional Galician dress rest in the shade at the annual Albariño Festival in Cambados, Galicia

helpful and allows you to find accommodation easily as well as offering general advice on what to do and where to go.

BODEGAS & MORE

RIBAS DE SIL
Pena das Donas
Avda de Galicia, 60
Entio B
27400 Monforte de Lemos
Tel 982 884 485
adega@penadasdonas.com
www.penadasdonas.com

SOBER
Adega Algueira
Doade s/n
27424 Sober
Tel: 982 152 238 or
629 208 917
info@adegaalgueira.com
www.adegaalgueira.com

MANZANEDA
Dominio do Bibei
Langullo s/n
32781 Manzaneda
Tel: 627 071 544
info@dominiodobibei.com
www.dominiodobibei.com

Ribeiro

East of Vigo on the A-52 you'll come to the heart of Ribeiro country, centered on Ribadavia. Set in lovely countryside the once so-so regional wine has in recent years become very much a talking point for quality white wine lovers the world over.

FOR FURTHER INFORMATION

Make sure you consult the local DO.
DO Ribeiro
Salgado Moscoso 11
32400 Ribadavia
Tel: 988 477 200
info@ribeiro.es
www.ribeiro.es

Leiro

Viña Mein
Lugar de Mein s/n
32420 Leiro.
Tel. 988 488 400
info.bodega@vinamein.com
www.vinamein.com

Bierzo

Roman naturalist Pliny the Elder (AD 23-79), mentioned the wines of Bergidum Flavium, today called Bierzo. Godello and Mencía wines here have achieved worldwide fame. The DO was founded in 1989.

At the Luna Beberide (founded 1987) in Cacabelos, Alejandro Luna, son of founder Bernardo, is enthusiastic about Godello. Their Mencía reds are also special.

Prada a Tope, based in the impressively restored Palacio de Canedo (circa 1730), has made a big effort to move to sustainable, organic viticulture. Its incredibly energetic owner, who introduces himself, with a firm handshake, simply as "Prada," began life as a shoemaker. Today he oversees a nationwide empire that includes restaurants, gastronomic retailing, a hotel, vineyards and a winery. Prada's red peppers are renowned throughout Spain; his wines also. A perfect place to eat and enjoy wines.

Bodegas y Viñedos Gancedo in Quilós was founded in 1998 to cultivate 13 hectares (32 acres) by Ginés Fernández López and his wife Juani Gancedo Hidalgo. They make some of the most delicate yet paradoxically powerful Godello going, blending in Doña Blanca to add depth. Incredibly, Ginés harvests from 63 lovingly tended individual

(JUAN MANUEL SANZ/ICEX)

Panniers filled with Mencía grapes in El Bierzo region, León

plots. The wines to try are Capricho and Herencia del Capricho.

FOR FURTHER INFORMATION
Contact either:
DO Bierzo
C/ Los Morales, 1, 2º
24540 Cacabelos
Tel: 987 549 408
info@crdobierzo.es
www.crdobierzo.es

or the very modern
Centro Para la Promoción de los vinos con DO Bierzo
C/ Mencía, 1
Campo de San Bartolo
24540 Cacabelos
Tel: 987 549 408
info@crdobierzo.es

BODEGAS & MORE

CACABELOS
Luna Beberide Antigua
Ctra Madrid-Coruña
Km 402, 24540 Cacabelos
Tel: 987 549 002
info@lunabeberide.es
www.lunabeberide.es

CANEDO
Prada a Tope
Viñedos y Bodegas del
Palacio de Canedo
C/ La Iglesia, s/n
24546 Canedo
Tel: 902 400 101
info@pradaatope.es
www.pradaatope.es
Call for reservations.

A Guarda, from Monte Santa Tecla

(PHILIP CLARK)

QUILÓS

Bodegas y Viñedos Gancedo
Parc 467, Pol 6, 24548
Cacabelos, Quilós
Tel: 987 134 980
or 676 984 085
info@bodegasgancedo.com
www.bodegasgancedo.com

Heading South

Valdeorras

The headquarters of DO Valdeorras, in the mountainside village of Villamartín de Valdeorras, is to a large extent the birthplace of the Godello and Mencía revolution that have had such an impact on modern Spanish wine. It is located on the N-120 between Ourense and León. A 1974 project called *Revival* recovered Godello from the brink of extinction and suggested planting Mencía (and is still working on other rare and almost extinct varieties). It was here that Godello was discovered to take on the aromas of fermentation and the nuances of terroir. Godello is not a terpenic grape like Albariño or Moscatel. **Godeval**, housed in a renovated old nunnery, was among the first to vinify modern Godello. As such it merits a visit. However, the rising star of the area is Rafael Palacios, brother of the Álvaro of Priorat fame. Rafael's winery is temporarily located in a modern suburban house but a new bodega is to be built next to some ancient stone terraces planted with selected vines. Try Louro (second wine) and the amazing As Sortes (top wine).

Val de Sil in Vilamatín de Valdeorras owns 26 hectares (64 acres), including amazing slate vineyards at 510 meters (1,670 ft) above sea level. The idea behind Montenovo is to express *terroir* at affordable prices. Val de Sil's Sobre Lías is more complex, full and rounded, while Pezas da Portela is fermented in oak and then passed to stainless steel to homogenize—a fabulous wine.

A Coroa is a winery which Roberto Fernández García's family has built within a restored 18th-century winery. Their wine is subtle and takes a while to open. At the other end of the scale is **Adega O Casal**, in Rubiá. It is a minimalist project aimed at expressing terroir to a maximum. Their label is Casal Novo.

FOR FURTHER INFORMATION
DO Valdeorras
Ctra N-120 Km 463
32340 Villamartín
Tel: 988 300 295
consello@dovaldeorras.com

BODEGAS & MORE

VILAMARTÍN DE VALDEORRAS
Bodegas Valdesil
C/ Córgomo s/n
32348 Vilamartín
de Valdeorras
Tel: 988 337 900
valdesil@valdesil.com
www.valdesil.com
Mon–Fri 9AM–1PM,
4PM–6PM
By prior arrangement.

A Coroa
LG Valenica do Sil s/n
32340 Vilamartín
de Valdeorras
Tel: 988 310 648
acoroa@acoroa.com
www.acoroa.com
Located on N-120
Km 465

O BARCO
Bodegas Godeval
Avenida de Galicia 20
32300 O Barco
de Valdeorras
Tel: 988 108 282
godeval@godeval.com
www.godeval.com

RUBIA
Adega O Casal
Pumarega 22
23210 Rubiá de Valdeorras
Tel: 988 342 067
casalnovo@casalnovo.es

WHERE TO STAY AND EAT

Leiro

Hotel Rural
Lugar de Mein s/n
32420 Leiro, Ourense
www.vinamein.com
Tel: 617 326 385
(Visitación Vázquez)
reservas.hotel@vinamein.com

Pontevedra

Parador el Albariño
Pº Calzada s/n
36630 Cambados
Pontevedra
Tel. 986 542 250
cambados@parador.es

Mesón Jaqueyvi
Doña Teresa, 1
36002 Pontevedra
Tel: 986 861 820
Good tapas at dinnertime.

Santiago de Compostela

Parador de los Reyes Católicos
Praza Obradoiro 1
15705 Santiago
de Compostela
Tel: 981 582 200 (H)

Anexo Vilas Avda
Villagarcía 21
Tel: 981 598 387
Traditional fare, well prepared. Pricey but splendid.
(R)

Casa Vilas
Rosalía de Castro 88
Tel: 981 591 000 (R)

Enxebre
Pl. del Obradoiro
Tel: 981 582 200 (R)

Tazas of Ribeiro wine

(ICEX)

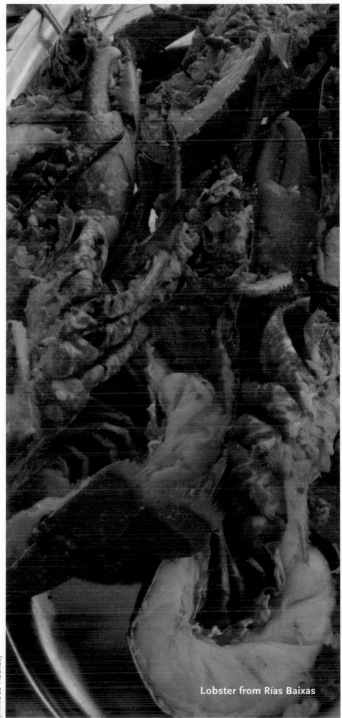

Lobster from Rías Baixas

THE BALEARIC &
CANARY ISLANDS

I T IS LIKELY THAT WINE CULTURE first entered Spain via its offshore islands through visits by Middle Eastern traders such as the Phoenicians. To this day the islands contain a treasure trove of rare and special grape varieties that provide a fascinating window on history. The Balearics, off the coast of Catalonia, and the Canaries, west of the North African coast, both retain important wine industries, albeit producing small volumes. There are records of winemaking in the Balearic Islands since the second century BC and Shakespeare refers to Canary wine in *The Merry Wives of Windsor*.

Tourism has had a major impact on the economic importance of winemaking on both island groups, providing the basis of a considerable renaissance. Today the Canary Islands produce a comprehensive array of extraordinary wines from no less than 11 denominated regions (12 if Fuerteventura is included). These are: DOs El Hierro; Gran Canaria; Monte Lentiscal; Vinos de la Gomera; La Palma; Lanzarote; Abona; Valle de Güímar; Valle de La Orotava; Tacoronte-Acentejo; and Ycoden-Daute-Isora.

Mallorca leads the way in the Balearics with two DOs: Binissalem-Mallorca and Plà i Llevant and subordinate regions called Vino de la Tierra Serra de Tramuntana-Costa Nord and Vino de la Tierra Mallorca. Vino de la Tierra classification also includes wines from Isla de Menorca, Ibiza and Formentera.

The Canaries are extraordinary because phylloxera has never infected vines there (unlike most of the rest of the world). Hence wines are harvested from a wealth of vines growing on their own roots, a scenario Julius Caesar would have recognised as his armies chased Pompey

《 A swimmer takes his body board out to catch waves among the surf on the northern coast of La Palma, Canary Islands

across Iberia. With the incorporation of modern vinification techniques white wines have reached quality levels only visible in Rías Baixas on the mainland.

The Balearics

Binissalem

Binissalem was set up in 1988 to promote winemaking from what now amounts to 600 hectares (1,480 acres) of vineyard, planted primarily with native Manto Negro and Moll.

There are currently 15 wineries active, and standout producers are **Macià**

Batle and **José L Ferrer**. Both are easily reachable by car from Palma taking the Ma-13 towards Inca. You must make appointments to visit.

Macià Batle
Camí de Coanegra s/n
07320 Santa Maria del Camí
Tel: 971 140 014
correo@maciabatle.com

José L Ferrer
Conquistador 103
07350 Binissalem
Tel: 971 511 050
bfroja.encata@bitel.es

Artichoke field in front of vineyards in Felanitx, Mallorca

FOR FURTHER
INFORMATION
**Consejo Regulador
DO Binissalem**
Ca'n Gelabert
Calle de la Concepció 7
07350 Binissalem
Tel: 971 886 577
Fax: 971 886 522
info@binissalemdo.com
www.binissalemdo.com

Plà i Llevant

Plà i Llevant boasts 12
wineries. Undenominated
wines made by **Ánima
Negra** are well worth seek-
ing out. They produce four
wines—An, AN/2, Quíbia,
and Son Negre—which
have attracted considerable
critical praise (although they
have been subject to vintage
variation). They don't
staff the winery unless a
specific visit request is made
by email. You'll find them
at: An Negra Viticultors
S.L., 3ª Volta, 18
A.P. 130
07200 Felanitx
info@annegra.com

FOR FURTHER
INFORMATION
DO Plà i Llevant
Molí de n'Amengual
carrer de Duzay
07260 Porreres
Tel: 971 168 569
Fax: 971 168 569
info@plaillevantmallorca.es
www.plaillevantmallorca.es

(HAROLD HECKLE)

(HAROLD HECKLE)

Bodega La Geria, Lanzarote, where winemaker Alejandro Besay offers wine to around 300,000 visitors annually

The Canaries

The Canaries combine a pristine environment, volcanic soils poor in organic matter, benevolent climate with perfect luminosity and some of the rarest vine varieties in the world. In short, a wine paradise. The island of Tenerife is a great place to begin a wine tour. Basically, if you drive anticlockwise around the island you'll enjoy some spectacular scenery as well as rare and often beautiful wine. The first DO you'll hit driving west from Santa Cruz de Tenerife is Tacoronte-Acentejo. It is here that the **Monje** family has a bodega and restaurant at **El Sauzal**; you'll see it as you drive to the town. Book a table overlooking the Atlantic and check out the wines. They are not necessarily the most modern island wines, but a good place to begin an acquaintance.

For a modern taste try **Buten**, whose Crater wine is a revelation and gives a real flavor of what volcanic soils can do.

Whatever you do, don't miss **Viñatigo** at the western tip of the island in

Ycoden-Daute-Isora. Wine quality here is world class, both white and red. Also, ask for their El Hierro wine; this is the only place you'll get a chance to buy some. El Hierro Baboso is among the great wines of Spain, and Vijariego Negro is not far behind.

The white (often dessert) wines of the islands of La Palma and Lanzarote are also worth searching for. Known for centuries as Canary Sack, it fortified many an intrepid sailor on the way to the New World, as the islands were the last glimpse of Europe they would see on sailing ships making use of the Atlantic's prevailing winds. You can take (more or less) cheap internal flights between islands.

You will notice potato fields planted on many different types of volcanic soils across the islands. Potatoes were landed on the Canary Islands before they were introduced to the rest of Europe (and the rest of the world) and there is nowhere outside their homeland in the Andes where they are more delicious. Don't miss them; they are called by their Andean name of "Papa." *Papas arrugadas* are boiled with skins on in seawater and are mouth-wateringly delicious. Often served with a mixture of island sauces called *Mojo* these potatoes with their crinkly skins delicately covered in sea salt are a rare delight. There are many varieties to try.

FOR FURTHER INFORMATION
Contact the islands' tourism board for help: www.turismodecanarias.com

(HAROLD HECKLE)

Baboso Negro vine in early bloom

Gran Canaria
Victor Hugo 60
35006 Las Palmas de
Gran Canaria
Tel: 928 293 698

Tenerife
Fomento 7—2a planta
Oficina 11-A
38003 Santa Cruz
de Tenerife
Tel: 922 229 466

BODEGAS & MORE

Monje
Calle Cruz De Leandro 36
38359 El Sauzal (Tenerife)
Tel: 922 585 027
monje@bodegasmonje.com
www.bodegasmonje.com

Buten
Calle San Nicolás 122
38360 El Sauzal
(Tenerife)
Tel: 922 573 272
crater@bodegasbuten.com
www.bodegasbuten.com

Viñatigo
Cabo Verde s/n
38440 La Guancha
(Tenerife)
Tel: 922 828 768
vinatigo@vinatigo.com
www.vinatigo.com

The white Marmajuelo
is spectacular, and don't
miss the red Negramoll or
Listán Negro.

Glasses of Engaja 2006, Bodegas
Carballo, Fuencaliente, La Palma,
Canary Islands; this grape variety is
known as Sercial in Madeira

(HAROLD HECKLE)

WHERE TO STAY AND EAT

Mallorca

Koldo Royo
Paseo Maritimo 3
07014 Palma de Mallorca
Tel: 971 732 435 (R)

**Wellies Restaurant
and Wine World**
Puerto Portals 23-24
Mallorca
Tel. 971 676 444
(Cristina Pérez)
cristina@wellies.es
www.wellies.es
A great restaurant with an
excellent wine shop.

(HAROLD HECKLE)

Tajinaste's Agustin Garcia trains a vine in DO Valle de La Orotava, Tenerife, where he and his son own six hectares

GLOSSARY OF USEFUL FOOD AND WINE TERMS

Aguardiente A strong transparent spirit distilled from wine.

Ajo Garlic.

Albariza The white soil of Jerez, with high limestone content.

Alcachofa Artichoke.

Allioli A popular garlic and olive oil sauce.

Amontillado Can be the most stunning of aged sherry or Montilla styles.

Arroz Rice.

Asado A roast.

Asador A restaurant specializing in roasted meats.

Bacalao Cod.

Barrica The classic Bordeaux-style 225-liter barrel, usually oak.

Bodega A winery or wine cellar.

Bodeguero The owner or manager of a bodega.

Brut or **Brut nature** A dry Cava.

Butifarra A Catalan or Balearic style of pork sausage.

Caldereta A stew, or the pot it is cooked in.

Callos Tripe.

Capataz A master taster or "foreman" in Jerez.

Cava Spain's sparkling wine par excellence, made in the traditional style. The name comes from the word *cava*, a cellar.

Chilindrón A type of sauce made from peppers, tomatoes and garlic, popular in Aragón, Navarra and the Rioja.

Chorizo A spicy pork sausage often with a hint of paprika spiciness.

Chuleta A chop. A *chuletón* is larger.

Cochinillo Suckling pig.

Codorniz Quail.

Conejo Rabbit.

Consejo Regulador The Regulating Council of a wine region, which enforces strict standards of quality and regional authenticity.

Catavino The traditional slender sherry glass, tapered in towards the mouth. Some people refer to it as a *copita* but this is the name given to any small glass.

Cordero Lamb.

Cosecha Vintage.

Cream A type of sherry or Montilla.

Criadera An oak butt used in the solera system.

Crianza A wine that has been aged in oak barrels.

Degüelle The disgorging process used for sparkling wines.

Dorada A type of fish popular in the Levante.

Dulce Sweet. Also used for a sweet type of Cava.

Estofado A stew.

Fino A clear, young dry sherry or Montilla.

Flor A fine layer of yeasts formed on the surface of the wine inside butts of sherry or Montilla. It helps protect the wine from oxidation and adds a hint of flavor.

Garnatxa d'Emporda A sweet dessert wine made in the Ampurdán.

Gazpacho In Andalusia this is a cold vegetable soup; in the Levante and La Mancha it is a hearty stew often made with snails.

Generoso A fortified apéritif or dessert wine.

Gran Reserva A traditional, usually expensive wine matured for many years in barrel and bottle. A bit antiquated now.

Habas Broad beans.

Horno (de asar) An oven.

Jamón Ham, one of Spain's major contributions to world gastronomy. From the simple, salted Serrano to the divine *Jabugo de Bellota*, don't miss out!

Judias Beans: *judias blancas* are haricot beans; *judias negras* are runner beans.

Licor de Tiraje A sweet wine added to sparkling wines in different measures to achieve different levels of sweetness.

Manzanilla A subtle, bone-dry sherry made in Sanlúcar de Barrameda, Jerez.

Masía A country house or winery in Catalonia.

Migas Breadcrumbs or flour fried in olive oil.

Morcilla A black sausage, akin to English black pudding.

Moscatel A sweet dessert wine made from the Moscatel grape.

Mosto Grape must or juice before fermentation.

Negre Catalan for "red wine."

Olla A stew pot.

Oloroso A type of sherry or Montilla. When aged, can be heavenly.

Paella The famous rice dish

from the Levante. Tradi-
tionally made with rabbit,
it can include meat, fish,
vegetables and thick-grain
rice, of which the Bomba
variety is the finest.

Pale Cream A type of sweet
sherry or Montilla.

Pálido Pale.

Palo Cortado A rare and
utterly divine type of
sherry. Sometimes a bit of
a mix between Amontil-
lado and Oloroso, but the
real thing is hard to find
and forget.

Parrillada A grill.

Patatas Potatoes.

Pato Duck.

Perdiz Partridge.

Petillante Slightly sparkling
or effervescent. Can also
be called *con aguja*.

Phylloxera A louse that
attacks and destroys the
roots of the vine. The
European industry has
defeated it by grafting
its stock onto resistant
American rootstock.

Picada A sauce made with
saffron, garlic, nuts, parsley and cinnamon.

Pimiento Pepper.

Pinchito A small kebab
usually served as a tapa.

Pintxo A Basque name for
some of the best bar snacks
in the world. Traditional
in northern Spain but sublime in the Basque region.

Queimada A Galician
blend of spirits, herbs
and even a touch of mag-
ic (called *el conjuro*) that is
set on fire and served in
little coffee-style cups.
Beware, deceptively
powerful.

Rancio An old white wine
that has been matured
and allowed to oxidize in
barrel.

Rape Hake.

Removido The turning
process used for sparkling
wine. The bottles are
gradually turned upside
down so that the sedi-
ment settles on the cork,
prior to its removal by
degüelle.

Reserva A high quality
wine that has been ma-
tured in barrel and bottle.

Revuelto de Setas A mushroom omelette.

Romesco A type of sauce
made with garlic, toma-
toes, peppers, bread and
almonds, very popular in
Catalonia.

Rosado Rosé wine.

Rovellón A type of wild
mushroom found in
Catalonia.

Samfaina A sauce made
with eggplant, tomatoes,
onions, and summer
squash.

Sangría A drink made with wine, brandy and fruit. Can provoke serious headaches if enjoyed with too much verve. A great way to ruin a wine.

Seco Dry. Also used to describe a medium dry Cava.

Sofrito A sauce of sautéed onions, tomatoes, peppers and garlic in olive oil.

Solera system The system used in the production of sherry, Montilla and Malaga. The *solera* is the butt of wine at ground level; the upper butts are known as *criaderas*.

Taninos Tannin, a mouth-puckering substance in the grape pips and stalks that gives the wine its backbone and staying power, enabling it to age longer.

Tapas Small dishes or appetizers served with drinks at a bar.

Ternera Veal.

Tinaja Large earthenware amphora-shaped containers in which wine is stored.

Torta A hard flour biscuit served with Gazpacho Manchego.

Tortilla An omelette.

Trucha Trout.

Varietal Wine made from a single grape variety.

Vendimia Grape harvest.

Vendimiador Grape picker.

Venencia A small thin silver cup attached to a whalebone; used by a *venenciador* to extract samples from the sherry butts and pour into glasses.

Vino Wine.

Vino de aguja Wine with a hint of *pétillance*.

Vino del año A wine intended to be consumed within a year of the harvest.

Vino del cosechero A wine produced by a small grape farmer, usually sold by the jug or demijohn.

Zarzuela A fish stew, particularly popular in Catalonia.

PRINCIPAL GRAPE VARIETIES

The following varieties are the principal grapes used in Spain:

Airén (white). The principal variety of Castilla La Mancha, Airén, can produce pleasant, light and fruity young whites, which are often rather neutral.

Albariño (white). Planted mostly in Galicia and producing wines with good acidity balanced with delicate, complex and often honeyed fruitiness. Tends to be rather low in aromas.

Bobal (black). A hardy vine planted mostly in Levante. Its wines tend to oxidize quickly, but it can produce good *rosados*.

Cabernet Sauvignon (black). One of the world's great travellers, and now one of the most popular imported "noble" varieties in Spain, planted increasingly in Navarra and Catalonia. South of the Pyrenees it produces enormous wines that are packed with color, fruit and tannin and thus are often blended with softer grape varieties.

Cariñena (black). Also known as Mazuelo, and planted in parts of Aragón and Catalonia with smaller pockets in Rioja. It produces wines that are deep in color, dry and with a high degree of alcohol and extract.

Cencibel. *See* Tempranillo.

Chardonnay (white). Another favorite import. In Spain it can produce some almost overpoweringly fruity and intense wines, but it is usually used in blends, to add a touch of finesse and depth to both still wines and Cavas.

Garnacha (black). An indigenous Spanish variety known in France as Grenache, this is now the most widely planted black variety in Spain, particularly in Navarra, Rioja and Aragón. When well vinified, it produces excellent, open and very fruity wines, so it is ideal for young reds and rosés. Its biggest weakness is its lack of tannin and staying power.

Garnacha Tintorera (black). The only grape with dark pulp as well as skin. Called Alicante Bouschet in some parts of Europe. Hard to vinify due to its propensity to oxidize.

Graciano (black). Planted in small parcels in Rioja Alta, it produces wines with good staying power, delicate aroma and flavor. Unfortunately, it is usually blended, but it can make a good blend into a really great one.

Macabeo. *See* Viura.

Malvasía (white). Planted in increasingly small parcels in Rioja, Navarra and the Canaries. It produces wines of character, with good body and aroma.

Mazuelo. *See* Cariñena.

Merseguera (white). Planted widely in Levante, particularly Valencia. Its pale wines can be fresh and fruity, but they tend to lack charm.

Monastrell (black). A favorite variety in Murcia.

Palomino (white). The great variety of Jerez, Palomino produces wines that lack character and are low in sugar and acidity. It is the solera system that transforms the unremarkable wines into excellent sherries.

Parellada (white). This is the best white variety in Catalonia, and particularly Penedès, where it produces wines of great freshness and crispness, with good fruit and aroma.

Pedro Ximénez (white). Widely planted in Montilla, and used in Jerez to make sweetening wines. It produces fairly neutral wines with a high level of alcohol (not surprisingly, considering the southern sun). Again, it is the solera system that transforms the wine.

Tempranillo (black). Also known as Ull de Llebre in Catalonia, and as Cencibel in New Castile and Levante. Tinto Fino of Ribera del Duero is a close variant as is Tinta de Toro. Usually considered to be the best native black variety of Spain, it is planted in increasing quantities all over the country. In Rioja it produces wines with good aroma, fruit and color. It blends well with Garnacha, which adds extra fruit and alcohol. Tempranillo provides the elegance and finesse.

Tinta de Toro. *See* Tempranillo.

Tinto Fino. *See* Tempranillo.

Ull de Llebre. *See* Tempranillo.

Verdejo (white). A native of Old Castile, increasingly planted in Rueda. Verdejo is capable of producing wines that are elegant, crisp, well-balanced, fruity and characterful.

Viura (white). Also known as Macabeo, and planted in Rioja, Navarra, Catalonia and Levante. Its wines are crisp, fruity and with good aroma, but they often lack character.

Xarel.lo (white). The third variety of Penedès, this grape produces wines that can be coarse, but they have body, acidity and a relatively high level of alcohol.

SPANISH VINTAGES

Spain has more hectares under vine than any other country in Europe, if not the world, and the grapes are grown in climatic conditions that vary considerably: the conditions in Jerez, for example, could not be more different than those in Ribera del Duero. It is therefore always difficult to generalize about Spain's vintages.

The weather is generally good for grape growing with the exception of potentially excessive heat during dry summers, which might cause vine stress, or rain during harvest time, which can promote mold, fungus and thin skins.

Each region has its own characteristics and an increasing number of wineries bottle terroir-specific wines. Traditionally, famous regions like Rioja have always blended wines from different areas, rendering vintages less meaningful. Recent trends have moved more in the direction of vineyard-specific wines, where local characteristics are far more visible.

Spanish red wines are generally only released when they are ready for drinking, having spent *crianza* aging in

	2008	2007	2006	2005	2004	2003
Priorat				E	E	VG
Rib de Due	VG	VG	G	VG	E	VG
Rioja	VG	VG	VG	E	E	G
Toro	E	VG	VG	E	E	E
Jumilla		G	VG	VG	E	VG

bodegas. This contrasts with French regions like Bordeaux or Burgundy where wines are sold *en primeur*, often years before they are drinkable.

High-quality Spanish wines tend to reach a plateau comparatively early, where stored properly they can stay for several years. The following vintage chart has been compiled from reports by the Consejos Reguladores, which classify their vintages from "excellent" to "poor" (though the latter category is rarely used). The chart is for red wines. Whites drink relatively early. This is a general guide only.

The ratings are Excellent, Very Good, Good and Poor.

FURTHER INFORMATION

WINES FROM SPAIN
www.winesfromspain.com
These are government run wine information and promotion bureaus and can be very helpful for advice, leaflets, addresses and general information:

UNITED STATES

Spanish Embassy—
Office for Economic & Commercial Affairs
405 Lexington Ave
44 Floor
New York, NY
Tel: 212 661 4959/60
www.winesfromspainusa.com

Chicago
500 North Michigan Ave
Ste 1500
Chicago, IL
Tel: 312 644 1154

Los Angeles
1900 Ave of the Stars
Ste 2430
Los Angeles, CA
Tel: 310 277 5125

Miami
2655 Le Jeune Rd, Ste 1114
Coral Gables, FL 33134
Tel: 305 446 4387

2002	2001	2000	1999	1998	1997	1996	1995
G	E	G	VG	E	G	E	E
VG	E	VG	F	VG	G	E	E
G	E	G	G	VG	G	VG	E
VG	E	VG	E	VG	G	VG	VG
G	G	VG	VG	E	G	VG	VG

Washington DC
2375 Pennsylvania Avenue
NW, Washington DC
Tel: 202 728 2368

UNITED KINGDOM:

UK Spanish Embassy—
Office for Economic &
Commercial Affairs
66 Chiltern St
Second Floor
London W1M 2LS
Tel: 207 467 2330
www.winesfromspainuk.com

CONSEJOS REGULADORES

Once you are in Spain,
Consejos Reguladores for each
Denomination of Origin
can prove helpful: they
provide information
leaflets and even personalized information. These
organizations are very busy
and sometimes do not have
English speakers at hand.
Each section in the book
contains information for its
Consejo.

TOURIST OFFICES

Spain receives some 60 million foreign tourists each
year and there are tour-
ist offices in most major
towns. These can be useful
for local information, and
they will usually be able
to provide travellers with

maps, lists of hotels, etc.

SPANISH NATIONAL TOURIST OFFICE

www.spain.info

UNITED STATES

New York
Tourist Office of Spain
666 Fifth Avenue, 35th Fl
New York, NY 10103
Tel: 212 265 8822
oetny@Tourspain.es

Los Angeles
8383 Wiltshire Blvd
Ste 956
Beverly Hills, CA 90211
Tel: 323 658 7188
losangeles@tourspain.es

Miami
1395 Brickell Ave, Ste 1130
Miami, FL 33131
Tel: 305 358 1992
oetmiami@tourspain.es

Chicago
845 North Michigan Ave
Ste 915-E
Chicago, IL 60611
Tel: 312 642 1992
chicago@tourspain.es

UNITED KINGDOM

PO Box 4009
London W1A 6NB
Twenty-four hour auto-
mated information and
brochure request line

084 59 400 180, information advisors 020 7486 8077 between 9:15AM and 1:30PM. info.londresa@tourspain.es

PARADORS

Spain's Paradors were once the ultimate in chic tourism. Many are set in magnificent locations, in castles and palaces. However, in the 21st century they have to compete with some remarkable opposition and sometimes they exude an old-style charm that can seem a bit dated. However, they do offer some fantastic deals (for example for those under 35 or over 55) that are well worthwhile checking out.

PUBLIC HOLIDAYS

Virtually every town and city in Spain celebrates the feast day of its patron saint and, if this day happens to be one day away from the weekend, the day in between also becomes a holiday (known as a *puente* or bridge). Most bodegas close during holidays, so it is very important to plan your trip ahead. Do call or send an email if in any doubt.

January 1
(New Year)
January 6
(Epiphany)

March 19
(St Joseph)
End March/early April
Maundy Thursday, Good Friday, Easter Monday (Easter usually amounts to an extended holiday)
May 1
(Labor Day)
Corpus Christi
(the second Thursday after Whitsunday)
July 25
(St James the Apostle)
August 15
(Ascension)
October 12
(Spain's national day, Our Lady of El Pilar)
November 1
(All Saints' Day)
December 8
(Immaculate Conception)
December 25
(Christmas and New Year tend to become an extended holiday)

USING THE TELEPHONE AND INTERNET IN SPAIN

If you do not have a cell phone with a roaming arrangement, it's best to buy a local chip, which you can do at airports or local mobile phone shops clearly visible in every major town and city.

Larger conurbations

have WiFi areas clearly marked out, and most airports have free WiFi areas. Some coffee houses also provide free WiFi services. Some outdoor kiosks also have open WiFi services, most of them free. Keep an eye out for WiFi signs. You can also ask locals, who may call it by its English name although sometimes it is also referred to as *wee-fee*.

SAMPLE LETTER (OR EMAIL) TO A BODEGA

[Sender's name, address, telephone and date]

Estimados Señores:

Tras leer A Traveller's Wine Guide to Spain *hemos visto que aceptan visitas. Estaremos en su región el día* [day] *de* [month] *de este año y nos gustaría, si no es inconveniente, visitar su bodega a las* [time].

Nos interesa mucho su región y quisiéramos conocer sus vinos y su estilo de vinificación.

Por favor respondan a nuestro correo electrónico para indicar si hay instrucciones especiales.

Agradeciéndoles de antemano su amable atención, les saluda muy atentamente

[signature]

Dear Sirs,

We have read in *A Traveller's Wine Guide to Spain* that you accept visits. We will be in your area on the [day] of [month] this year and would like to visit your winery at [time].

We are very interested in your region and would like to know more about your wines and how they were made.

Please reply to our email address and indicate if there are any special instructions.

Thanking you in advance for your kind attention.

[signature]

FURTHER READING

TRAVEL AND HOTEL GUIDES

Guía Campsa (revised frequently). A guide to the country's best hotels and restaurants, published by Spain's national gas company, available in airports and bookshops. In Spanish.

The Cadogan Guides (revised annually). Excellent for up-to-date

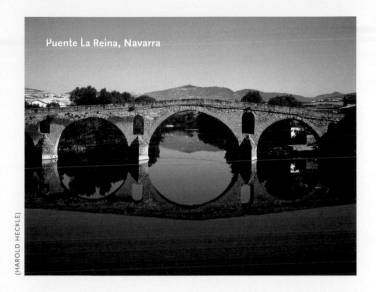

Puente La Reina, Navarra

(HAROLD HECKLE)

information on everything you need on the road. Visit www.interlink-books.com

The Rough Guide to Spain (www.roughguides.com) An excellent and well-researched guide to off-beat travel in Spain.

WRITERS' TRAVEL BOOKS

These are some of the most compelling travel companions:

Gerald Brenan *South from Granada*, and *The Spanish Labyrinth*. Both books are excellent reading—including marvelous descriptions of village life near Granada in the 1920s and 1930s.

Ernest Hemingway *Death in the Afternoon*. One of the most fascinating books to have been written about Spain by an outsider, a must for anyone who is interested in bullfights.

Laurie Lee *As I Walked Out One Midsummer's Morning*, *A Rose for Winter*, *A Moment of War*. Beautifully written books relating the writer's travels in Spain in the 1930s and 1950s, giving a lovely and loving glimpse of the country from a time that has vanished but whose imprint is likely to be eternal.

Jan Morris *Spain*. A perceptive and excellent book full of wonderfully descriptive passages.

Chris Stewart *Driving Over Lemons*. A delightful modern-day description of quirky rural life.

INDEX

A Coroa, 169
A Guarda, 162
Aalto, 88-9
Abadía Retuerta, 87, 89
Adega Algueira, 164-5
Adega O Casal, 169
Agnusdei, 161, 163
Agro de Bazán, 161, 163
Aguilar de la Frontera, 118, 123
Ainzón, 46
Airén grape, 120; *see also* Layrén
Albariño grape, 155, 157-8, 161-3,
  168, 170
albariza, 118, 122, 131-2, 140
Alella, xiv, 57, 60-1
Alella Vinícola, 60
Alfaro, 12, 25, 38
Alicante, xiv, 111, 184
Alquézar, 43, 47
Alvear S.A., 123
Amontillado, 118-20, 124, 130-3, 145, 182
Ampurdán-Costa Brava, 57, 59-60,
  77, 181
Andalusia (Andalucía, Al-Andaluz,
Al-Andalus), 81, 98, 115-49, 181
Antequera, 124-125
Antonio Barbadillo S.A., 141, 143, 145
Aragon, 5, 12-13, 26, 40-7, 54, 56, 63,
  81, 95, 180, 184
Arcade, 161-2
Arcos de la Frontera, 129
Arnedillo, 25, 38
asadores, 8, 25, 38
autopistas, xxiii, 25
Ayegui, 10, 12

Baja Montaña, 5
Baladí grape, 120
Balearics, 173-9
Barbadillo, see Antonio Barbadillo
Barbastro, 41-3, 45, 47
Barcelona, 3, 41, 51-3, 56, 59-60, 63,
  71, 78, 111
Batalla del Vino, 36
Benalmadena, 125
Binissalem, 173-5
Bodega Antiqua Casa de Guardia, 126
Bodega Casa de la Ermita, 106, 109
Bodega Julia Roch e Hijos, 108
Bodega Numanthia Termes, 91-2
bodegas, x-xi, xiv-xv, 190

Bodegas Alejandro Fernández, 88-9
Bodegas Balcona, 110-11
Bodegas Bilbaínas, 34
Bodegas Carchelo Paraje, 109
Bodegas Castaño, 111-12
Bodegas Castro Martín, 161
Bodegas Contino, 30, 33
Bodegas El Nido, 109-10
Bodegas Escudero, 25-6
Bodegas Fernández de Piérola, 27
Bodegas Franco-Españolas, 26
Bodegas Godeval, 168-9
Bodegas Guelbenzu, 11-12
Bodegas Irache, 10, 12
Bodegas Irius, 44
Bodegas Jorge Ordóñez, 126
Bodegas José L. Ferrer, 174
Bodegas Julián Chivite, 11-3
Bodegas Lalanne, 44
Bodegas Laus, 44-5
Bodegas Luzón, 109
Bodegas Málaga Virgen, 126-7
Bodegas Marqués de Murrieta,
  26-7, 161
Bodegas Martínez Bujanda, 27-8
Bodegas Miguel Merino, 32
Bodegas Monasterio, 88-9
Bodegas Muga, 34-5
Bodegas Olarra, 26-7
Bodegas Ontañon, 26
Bodegas del Palacio de Fefiñanes, 161-2
Bodegas Palacio Remondo, 25
Bodegas Pazo de Barrantes, 161, 163
Bodegas Pingus, 88
Bodegas Pirineos, 43, 45
Bodegas Principe de Viana, 7, 15
Bodegas Protos, 87, 89
Bodegas Raimat, 71
Bodegas Riojanas, 31, 33
Bodegas Salnesur, 161
Bodegas de Sarría, 10, 13
Bodegas Torres, 63-5, 68, 71, 74, 76
Bodegas Valdesil, 169
Bodegas Vilariño-Cambados, 161
Bodegas y Viñedos Gancedo, 168
Bodegas y Viñedos Maurodós, 92
Bodegas y Viñedos Pintia, 92
Bodegas Ysios, 29, 33
Bordeaux, 3, 22-4, 31, 44, 106, 180, 187
Borja, 12, 46
brandy, 37, 77, 134-5, 140, 162, 183

Brandy de Jerez, 134-5
Briones, 32
bullfighting, 87, 99, 129, 144
Burgundy, 187
Buten, 176, 178

Cabernet Sauvignon grape; Aragon, 41, 43-5; Catalonia, 65; Murcia, 106 7, 109-11; Navarra, 6-7; New Castile, 85; Old Castile, 85
Cadaqués, 57 9
Cádiz, 129-30, 139
Caiño grape, 158
Calahorra, 25, 38
Cambados, 153, 161-2, 170
Campo de Borja, 12, 46
Can Ràfols dels Caus, 65, 68
Canaries, 173-9, 185
Canedo, 166-7
Capmany, 57
Cariñena, 46, 65
Cariñena grape, 57; see also Mazuelo
Casa Castillo, 110
Cascante, 11-12
Castilla La Mancha, see New Castile
Castilla-León, see Old Castile
Castrelo, 161
Catalonia, 41, 49-79
Cataluña, 57
Cava, 51, 55-7, 61-3, 65, 70
Cava Bodega, 65
Cenicero, 6-7, 31-3, 36
Centro Para la Permoción de los Vinos, 167
Chardonnay grape, 25, 41, 44, 65, 110, 123, 158
Cigales, 85
Cintruénigo, 11-12, 15
claretes, 23
Codorníu, 66-9, 71-2
Compañía Vinícola del Norte de España (C.V.N.E.), 30, 33-5
Conca de Barberá, 57, 65
Condado de Haza, 88-9
Condado do Tea, 153, 157, 162
Consejos Reguladores, xix, 63, 87, 131-2, 135, 139, 160, 175, 187-8
cooperatives, 43, 58-60, 62, 71, 155
copitas, 132
Córdoba, 116-20, 138, 144, 147
cosecha, xxi, 180
Costa de la Luz, 127-8
Costa del Sol, 115, 125, 127
Costers del Segre, 57, 69

Cream sherry, 121, 124, 131, 136
criadera, 134
crianza, xix-xx, 6, 88, 91, 106-7, 131, 186
Croft, see Rancho Croft
Cuéllar, 95
C.V.N.E., see Compañía Vinícola del Norte de España

deguelle, 56
Denominaciónes de Origen (D.O.s), xiv, xxi
Domecq, see Pedro Domecq
Dominio do Bibei, 164-5
Doña Blanca, 163
driving, roads, x, xxi-xxiv
Duff Gordon & Co., 136

El Bierzo, 156, 166-7
El Molino, 138
Elciego, 30-31
Emilio Lustau S.A., 142
Enate Viñedos y Crianza del Alto Aragón, 45
Espolla, 57
Estella, 10
EVENA, 11

Falset (Montsant), 71, 74
Federico Paternina S.A., 35
Félix Callejo, 88-9
Feria de San Fermín, 3, 7, 13
Feria de San Mateo, 37
Fernando A. de Terry, 140
festivals: Andalusia, 117, 125, 129, 144-5; Murica, 110; Navarra, 3, 7, 13; Old Castile, 99; Rioja, 36-7
Figueres, 59
Fino, 120, 123, 130-3, 141, 143, 145
food: Andalusia, 140-1, 143-9; Balearic & Canary, 177-9; Catalonia, 59-60, 76-9; Galicia, 170; Murcia, 112-3; Navarra, 7, 13-15; New Castile, 94-101; Old Castile, 83-4; Rioja, 34-9
Fornelos, 152, 163
Freixenet, 67
Fuendejalón, 46
Fuenmayor, 28

Galicia, 26, 151-71, 184
Garnacha grape; Aragon, 41, 44; Catalonia, 57, 74; Navarra, 5-6; Rioja, 21-2, 25
Garnacha Blanca grape, 21, 57
Garnacha Tintorera grape, 111, 155

Garró grape, 65
generosos, 1
girasoles, 56
Godello grape, 151, 154-5, 163-4, 166, 168
González Byass, 44, 135-8, 142, 144-5
Graciano grape, 23, 103
Gramona, 68
Gran Bodega Tio Pepe, 138
Gran Canaria, 173, 178
gran reserva, xix-xx, 44, 56, 135
Granada, 115-116, 144, 192
Granja Fillaboa, 162, 163
Grávalos, 25, 26
Guwürztraminer grape, 41, 44, 158

Haro, 25, 33-8, 110
Harvey, see John Harvey B.V.
Hemingway, Ernest, 3, 7,129, 192
holidays, public, 189
hornos de asar, 97
hotels, xv-xvii, 190-1
Huesca, 41
Huguet de Can Feixes, 65

insurance, xxiii-xxiv
internet, xxv, 189-90
Irache, 10

Jean León, 64
Jerez de la Frontera, xiv, 118, 127,
   129-42, 144, 147, 186
John Harvey B.V., 136, 142
Jumilla, 103, 105, 108-113

La Bleda, 67-8
La Concha, 138
La Granja Nuestra Señora de
   Remelluri, 30, 33
La Mancha, 135
La Oliva, 11
La Palma, 173, 177
La Rioja Alta S.A., 34-5, 162
Lagar de Cervera, 162-3
Lagar de Fornelos, 162-3
Laguardia, 28-30, 33
Lanzarote, 173, 177
Las Campanas, 9, 12
Layrén (Airén) grape, 120
Leiro, 166, 170
Levante, 181-2, 184-6
Logroño, 19-20, 26-7, 36-7, 39
López de Heredia, 34-5
Loureira grape, 155, 157, 163
Luis Caballero, 140

Luna Beberide, 166-7
Lustau, *see* Emilio Lustau

Macabeo grape, 62, 185-6; *see also* Viura
Macià Batle, 174
Madrid, 90, 93-6, 115
Magallón, 46
Málaga,117, 124-7, 131, 143, 147
Malbec grape, 85
Mallorca, 173, 179
Malvasía grape, 21
Manto Negro grape, 174
Manzanilla, 130-1, 141
Marqués de Alella, 60
Marqués de Cáceres, 31
Marqués de Riscal, 30-1, 33, 86, 92-3
Masía Bach, 67
Mazuelo grape (Samsó), 21; *see also*
   Cariñena grape
Mencía grape, 151, 154, 166-8
Medina del Campo, 84-5, 90, 95
Méntrida, 68
Merlot grape, 6, 43-5, 65, 85, 107, 110
meseta, 81
Moll grape, 174
Mollet, 57
Monastrell grape, 105-6, 108-12
Monje, 176, 178
Monte Santa Tecla, 162
Montilla (town), 117-8, 122-3, 131, 148
Montilla (wine), 118-24, 143
Montilla-Moriles, xiv
Montsant, see Falset
Moriles, 118, 131
Moristel grape, 41, 43
Moscatel grape, 126-7, 131
Mourvedre grape, 105
Murcia, 103-113
museums, wine: Andalusia, 139;
   Catalonia, 63; Navarra, 8;
   New Castile, 87, 89; Old Castile, 87,
   89; Rioja, 32

Navarra, 3-15, 41, 56
New Castile, 81-101, 184

O Rosal, 153, 157, 161-2
Ochoa, 7
Old Castile, 81-101
Olite, 10-1, 15
Ollauri, 33-34
Oloroso, 118-22, 124, 130-3, 146
Oro de Castilla, 93-4
Osborne S.A., 136, 140, 142, 145

Oyón, 26-8

paella, 77
Pago de Carraovejas, 88-9, 97
Palma de Mallorca, 179
Palo Cortado, 124, 130, 133, 146
Palomino grape, 130-2, 151, 155
Pamplona, 3, 7-9, 13, 15
Paradores, xvii, 189
Parellada grape, 62
Parraleta Grape, 41, 43
Parxet, 60-61
passport, xxiii
Pazo San Mauro, 162-3
Pedraza de la Sierra, 95
Pedro Domecq S.A., 135, 138, 141,
  144-5
Pedro Ximénez grape, 118-23, 126-7,
  132, 146
Pedrosa del Rey, 92
Pena das Donas, 163, 165
Peñafiel, 84, 87, 89-90
Penedès, 56-7, 61, 65-6, 74
Perelada, 59, 61-4
Pérez Barquero, 124
Pesquera, 88-9
Petit Verdot, 107, 110
phylloxera, 23, 26, 44, 49-51, 54-5, 57,
  61, 85, 105, 126, 151, 155, 173
Pineau, Jean, 31
Pla del Bages, 57
Plà i Llevant, 173, 175
Pont de Molins, 57
Pontevedra, 161, 163, 170
Porrera, 71, 74, 76
Praia a Lanzada, 161
Prada a Tope (Viñedos y Bodegas
  del Palacio de Canedo), 166-7
Priorat, 57, 71-5, 168
Pueblos Blancos, 128
Puente la Reina, 5, 9-10, 13, 15
Puerto de Santa Maria, 130, 132,
  139-40, 148

Quel, 25
Quilós, 168
Quintanilla, 89, 94

Raimat, 69-71
Rancho Croft, 136
Raventós i Blanc, 65, 68
removido process, 56
reserva, xix-xx, 6, 45, 88, 135
restaurants, xvii-xviii

Rey Fernando de Castilla, 142
Rías Baixas, 151-3, 156-8, 160, 174
Riaza, 95
Ribadavia, 154, 166
Ribadumia, 161, 163
Ribas de Sil, 165
Ribeira Sacra, 151-4, 156, 163-5
Ribeiro, 153-4, 156, 166
Ribera Alta, 5, 7
Ribera Baja, 5
Ribera del Duero, 56, 85-7, 90, 97, 186
Ricardell, 57
Rioja, xxi, 6, 13, 17-39, 83, 86, 92-3,
  103, 181, 186
Rioja Alavesa, 17-9, 21-2, 27-9
Rioja Alta, 17-22, 28-35, 152
Rioja Baja, 17-9, 21, 24-5
Roa, 88-9
roads, driving, x, xxi, xxiv
Ronda, 128-9, 148
rosados, 5-6, 24, 86
Rovellats, 68
Rubía, 169
Rueda, 86, 92-3
Ruta del Vino, 41, 43, 158-9

Salvaterra de Miño, 153, 162-3
San Román de la Hornija, 92
Sandeman, 136-42
Sanlúcar de Barrameda, 131-2, 140-3, 149
Sant Esteves Sesrovires, 67
Sant Martí Sarroca, 66, 68
Sant Sadurní d'Anoia, 66-8
Santa Daría, 31, 36
Santiago de Compostela, 3, 151,
  159-60, 170
Sardón de Duero, 89
Sauvignon Blanc grape, 93, 123
Scala Dei, 72, 76
Scholtz Hermanos, 126
Segovia, 95-7, 100
Segura Viudas, 69
Sepúlveda, 95, 100
Seville, 144
sherry, 117-27, 129-41, 143, 151, 155
'Sherry Triangle', xiv, 127, 129-35
solera system, 121, 132-5
Somontano, 41-2
Sotillo de la Ribera, 88-9
sparkling wine (Rueda Espumoso),
see Cava
Subirats, 68
Syrah grape, 74, 106-11

Tabuenca, 46
Tacaronte-Acentejo, 173, 176
Tafalla, 10-1, 13
tapas, xvii-xviii
Tarragona, 57, 63, 71, 77-9
telephone, 189-90
Tempranillo grape (Cencibel, Ull de Llebre); Aragon, 43-5; Castille, 85, 90; Murcia, 107, 110; Navarra, 6-7; Rioja, 19-21, 29
Tenerife, 176, 178
Terra Alta, 57
Tierra Estella, 5, 7
tinajas, 121
Tinta de Toro grape, 85, 90
Tinto Fino (Tinto del País) grape, 85
Tordesillas, 84, 90, 93, 95, 99-100
Toro, 85-6, 90-2
Toro Albalá, 124
Torre de Oña, 35
Torrelavit, 69
Torremolinos, 125
Torrontés grape, 120, 163
tourist offices, 188
Treixadura grape, 155, 158, 163
Tudela, 9, 11, 15, 87
Tui, 153, 162

Ujué, 11, 15
Unión Viti-Vinícola, Bodegas Marqués de Cáceres, 33
Utiel-Requena, 56

Val do Salnés, 157, 161
Valbuena de Duero, 88-9

Valdefinjas, 92
Valdeorras, 154, 168-9
Valdepeñas, 115
Valdizarbe, 5
Valencia, 103
Valladolid, xiv, 81-5, 90, 100-1
Valle de Güímar, 173
Valle de la Orotava, 173
Vega Sicilia, 85, 89-90
Verdejo grape, 93
Vilafranca del Penedès, 63, 66, 68-9
Vilanova de Arousa, 161, 163
Viña Mein, 166
Viñas del Vero, 43, 45, 47
Viñatigo, 176, 178
Viñedos del Contino, 33
Vinícola Hidalgo y Cia S.A., 141, 143
Vinícola Navarra, 9, 12
Vino Joven, xix, xxi, 22, 106, 122
Vino de la Tierra, 173
vintages, xvi, 186-7
Viura grape, 6-7, 62, 93; *see also* Macabeo
Williams & Humbert, 136, 139, 142
wine: aging, classification, labels, xiv, xvii-xxi, 186

Xarello grape, 62

Ycoden-Daute-Isora, 173, 176
Yecla, 103, 111-3

Zaragoza, 41-3

(HAROLD HECKLE)

Dormant volcano Teide on the Canary Island of Tenerife as seen from La Gomera